ClarisWorks 2.1 *for Macintosh*

Visual QuickStart Guide

ClarisWorks 2.1

for Macintosh

by Adam Greif

ClarisWorks 2.1 for Macintosh:
Visual QuickStart

Peachpit Press, Inc.
2414 Sixth Street
Berkeley, CA 94710

Cover Design: Studio Silicon

Distribution
Peachpit Press books are distributed to the U.S. book trade by Publishers Group West, 4065 Hollis, P.O. Box 8843, Emeryville, CA 94609, phone: 800/788-3123 or 510/658-3453, fax: 510/658-1834. Peachpit books are also available from wholesalers throughout the U.S. including Baker & Taylor Books, Golden-Lee Book Distributors, and Ingram Book Company. Resellers outside the book trade can contact Peachpit directly at 800/980-8999.

Author:
Adam Greif is a journalist living in Paris, France, who has written several books about the Macintosh in French and English.
He can be reached at the AppleLink address: Greif.

Thanks:
To Kristin Barendsen for her very careful reading of this book.

ISBN: 1-56609-122-5

0 9 8 7 6 5 4 3 2 1

Printed and bound in the United States of America

PRINTED ON RECYCLED PAPER

Contents

ClarisWorks is an *Integrated Software* program. It lets you create and mix several "types" of documents.

This book describes version 2.1 of ClarisWorks, which has two more features than version 2.0: *Mail* and *Hyphenation.*

PRELIMINARY

Macintosh Basics	2
Install	4

TEXT

Basics

Page	8
Word	10
Paragraph	12
Tabs, Invisibles	14

Menus

Apple:	Help	16
File:	New	18
	Open, Save	20
	Shortcuts	22
	Macros	24
	Mail	26
	Print	28
Edit:	Cut & Paste	30
	Spelling, Find	32
	Publish/Subscribe	34
Format		36
Font/Size/Style		38
Outline:	Basics	40
	Collapse, Edit	42
View:	Scale	44
	Tile, Stack, New	46
	Slide Show	48

DRAW

Basics

Tools	52
Palettes	54
Objects	56

Menus

Edit	58
Format	60
Arrange	62
Options: Master Page	64
Info, Text Wrap	66

PAINT

Basics

Tools	70

Menus

Format	74
Transform	76
Options	78

SPREADSHEET

Basics

Cell	82
Formulas	84
Charts	86
Chart Gallery	88

Menus

Edit/Format		90
Calculate:	Fill	92
	Sort, Insert	94
Options		96

DATABASE

Basics

Records	100
Browse	102
Find	104
Layout Mode	106
Columnar Layout	108
Calculation	110
Summary	112

Menus

Layout: Info, Slide	114
Field Options	116
Organize	118

COMMUNICATIONS

Settings	122
Session/Keys	126

EXAMPLES

Tables	130
Mail Merge	134
DTP	136

APPENDIX

Functions	142
Shortcuts	146
Index	151

If you are discovering
ClarisWorks and
the Macintosh computer
at the same time,
you should first read
the manuals that
come with your
Macintosh in order
to understand
files, folders,
menus, etc.
The two first *Preliminary*
pages sum up some of these
Macintosh basics. You do not need to study
them if you already know the Macintosh.
The two next pages describe the way to install
ClarisWorks from its original floppy disks onto your
Macintosh's hard disk. You can skip them if
ClarisWorks is already installed on your Macintosh.

PRELIMINARY

What you see on the screen when you turn on the Macintosh is called the *Desktop*. Electronic *Files* and *Folders* evoke the paper files and folders you shuffle on a wooden desk.

The first picture below shows the *Catalog window* of a hard disk called "Macintosh HD." The hard disk's files and folders are represented by *Icons*.

The *Menu bar* above the desktop lets you pull down *Menus* and choose *Commands*. Choosing a command followed by an ellipsis (i.e. three dots...) displays a *Dialog box* requesting some info. In this book, menu names and commands are written in **bold** letters.

ICONS

This window contains five folder icons, including one for a *Shared* folder which you can open from another network Macintosh.

The "Old Stuff" icon is highlighted (inverted), indicating that the Old Stuff folder is *selected* for action. You might open it, or duplicate it, or delete it. "ClarisWorks" is an *Application program*, or an *Application*. "Budget" is a *Document* created with this application.

CLOSE BOX

Clicking this box closes the window.
This is similar to choosing the **Close** command in the **File** menu.

TITLE BAR

Click and drag this bar to move the window around.

ZOOM BOX

Clicking this box makes the window big enough to show all its contents or fill the screen, or brings it back to its original size.

SCROLL BAR

In this example, some icons are hidden outside the window, and you might want to scroll them into sight.
Click the scroll bar *Arrows* for a slow scroll; drag the *Scroll Box* for a fast one. Click above or under the Scroll Box to scroll by one full window length.

POINTER

The black arrow is the *Pointer*. It is driven by the mouse.

SIZE BOX

Dragging this box lets you change the size of the window.

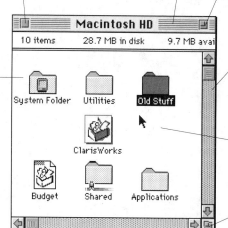

MOUSE

To *click* means "to press and release the mouse button."
To *drag* means "to move the mouse while its button is down."
When a key like Shift or Option is pressed at the same time, MacSpeak verbs are used: *Shift-click, Option-click, Shift-drag, Option-drag*, etc.

As you'll notice, the Macintosh keyboard has more keys than a typewriter keyboard. Their uses are explained below.

The keyboard below is that of a standard Macintosh LC. The location of some keys may be different on other models.

The *extended* keyboard, which usually comes with Quadras, features still more keys for shortcuts.

TAB
In the Text module of ClarisWorks, pressing the Tab key sends the Insertion Point to the next Tab stop.
In Spreadsheet mode, the Tab key validates an entry and moves the Pointer to the next cell.
In Database mode, it sends the Insertion Point to the next text field.
The Tab key also sends the Insertion Point to the next field inside dialog boxes.

BACKSPACE/DELETE
Pressing this key deletes the last letter you typed—or whatever text, picture or element is selected.

RETURN
This key inserts a *hard return* or *paragraph character* into text.
In Spreadsheet mode, it lets you validate an entry and move down one cell.
In a dialog box, it is equivalent to the Enter key (see below).

CAPS-LOCK

SHIFT

CONTROL
This key is used in some keyboard shortcuts (in the Text module's Outlining mode).

OPTION
This key lets you type special characters, like {, ®, π, ©, ≠, ¥, etc.
It is also used in keyboard shortcuts.

COMMAND
This key is often called the *Apple* key by ignoramuses, but it is officially the *Command* key.
Pressing it and typing a letter lets you choose a command without pulling down a menu. Such *shortcuts* are shown inside the menus as, for example, ⌘**A**.

ESCAPE
This key lets you cancel an entry in Spreadsheet mode.

ARROWS
These keys let you move the Insertion Point in text, the Pointer in a spreadsheet, or a selected Draw or Paint picture on the page.

ENTER
This key lets you validate an entry in Spreadsheet mode. In a dialog box, it is a shortcut for a click on a thick-bordered button marked *OK, Open,* etc.

PRELIMINARY

If ClarisWorks is already installed on your hard disk, you can skip these two pages.

Installing the program yourself is quite easy. Insert the first floppy disk into the drive of your Macintosh and double-click the Installer icon.

Claris advises you to turn off any anti-virus program before you install. One way to do this is to restart your Macintosh and hold the Shift key down until you see a panel saying "Welcome to Macintosh. Extensions off."

INSTALLER
Double-click this icon to display the dialog box below and start the installation process.

CLARISWORKS.SIT
The "sit" part means "Stuff-It," the name of a program that was used to *compact* the file. The installation process will "unstuff" it.
The "Read Me" document contains late-breaking information.

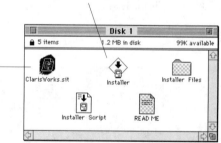

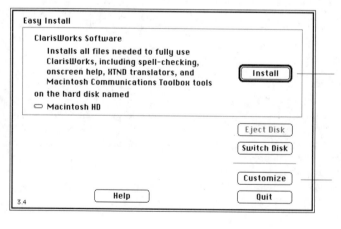

INSTALL
The program copies and unstuffs files from the first floppy disk, then asks you to insert the second one.

CUSTOMIZE
Clicking this button changes the dialog box into the one shown on the opposite page.

When you open ClarisWorks for the very first time, a dialog box asks for your name, company and serial number. This is a kind of symbolic protection against software piracy: you shouldn't install a program labeled with somebody else's name on your Macintosh. There is no barrier against such an installation, but it is forbidden by copyright law.

If the small international school used as an example in this book has five Macintosh computers and wants to use ClarisWorks on all of them, it should buy five programs, or ask Claris for a special license.

Note that two copies of the same ClarisWorks located on a network won't open at the same time.

CUSTOMIZE

Easy Install requires two megabytes of hard disk space. Minimum custom installation (installing only the ClarisWorks application) requires 600K.
The Tutorial goes along with the "Getting Started" manual.
Sample documents are worth leafing through at least once.
Help is a must (see p. 17).
Some files are installed in a folder called ClarisWorks 2.0, others in a folder called Claris inside the System folder.

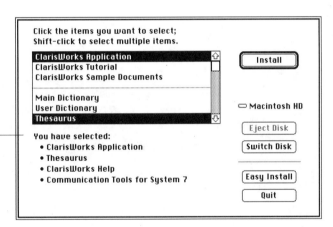

Click the items you want to select;
Shift-click to select multiple items.

- ClarisWorks Application
- ClarisWorks Tutorial
- ClarisWorks Sample Documents

- Main Dictionary
- User Dictionary
- Thesaurus

You have selected:
- ClarisWorks Application
- Thesaurus
- ClarisWorks Help
- Communication Tools for System 7

Install

⊟ Macintosh HD

Eject Disk

Switch Disk

Easy Install

Quit

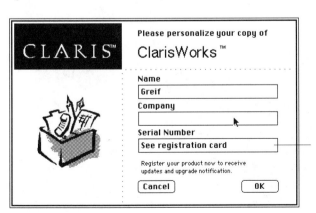

CLARIS™

Please personalize your copy of
ClarisWorks™

Name
Greif

Company

Serial Number
See registration card

Register your product now to receive updates and upgrade notification.

Cancel   OK

REGISTRATION
The Registration card is hidden inside a small booklet called "Why Bother?"

Text

AText is ClarisWorks' default document type. When you open ClarisWorks and do not specify otherwise, a blank text document appears on the screen. Text menus are the backbone of ClarisWorks. Menus in other modes include most text commands, plus mode-specific commands. Although ClarisWorks lacks some refinements of dedicated word processing programs (you can't create an index, for example), it has three features that make it superior in some situations to mighty Microsoft Word:

- You can draw pictures and create tables right inside a Text document's window.

- You can start from a Draw mode document, then create Text "frames" inside it to use ClarisWorks for desktop publishing (DTP).

- You can link Text and Database documents to create form letters through the process of "mail merge."

TEXT BASICS

When the Einstein International School decided to go modern and buy computers, they bought as much hardware as their budget allowed, but they didn't give much thought to software. Obviously, they needed a word processing program to write mail and reports to the trustees. They needed a spreadsheet program to keep track of the budget, and a database to store names and addresses of pupils. They intended to communicate by modem with their sister school in Purdue, Indiana.

ClarisWorks was an obvious choice: it would fit much better within the budget than would separate programs, and its ability to insert tables and graphs easily into reports would prove valuable.

The school could produce a newsletter, organize mailings, and send electronic mail—all with one program!

SIX PROGRAMS IN ONE

When you create a new document by double-clicking the ClarisWorks icon or by choosing the **New...** command in the **File** menu, this dialog box offers you a list of six types. *Word Processing* is the default option.

You can also create a new document by duplicating an existing one or by opening a "Stationery" file (see p. 21).

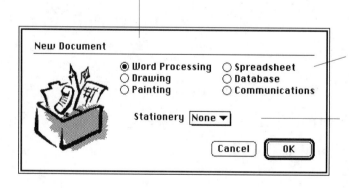

TAB

In this dialog box, pressing the Tab key or the Down arrow key selects the next "type."

STATIONERY

The pop-up menu lists stationery documents located in the *ClarisWorks Stationery* folder (located inside the Claris folder inside the System folder).

The word processing mode of ClarisWorks is similar to a dedicated word processing program. The main difference is that it is simpler, which is not a bad thing if you are a Macintosh beginner.

HEADER
Text written here appears on top each page.
A new document has no Header (or Footer).
Choose **Insert Header** (or **Insert Footer**) in the **Format** menu to create one.

MARGIN
The white, non-printing part of a page is separated from the work area by lines called "page guides."

I-BEAM POINTER
This is what the mouse-driven pointer looks like over a text zone. It reverts to its arrow shape over the scroll bar or the menu bar.

FIRST-LINE INDENT
The first line of this paragraph begins 1/2 inch to the right of the margin. Such paragraph attributes are easily defined on the ruler.

PARAGRAPH
When text reaches the right margin, it flows automatically to the next line. The Return key is used only to create a new paragraph.

RULER
There is a similar ruler on typewriters—you use it to shape what you are going to type.
On a computer, you can also shape what you have already typed.

WP
"WP" indicates that the document belongs to the word processing mode.

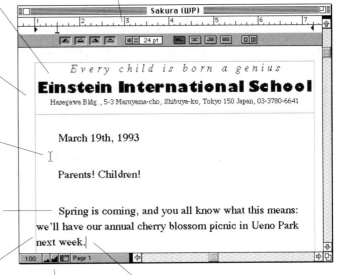

VIEW CONTROLS
From left to right:
Zoom percentage,
Zoom in and out buttons, Show/Hide tools button.

INSERTION POINT
This blinking bar shows where a typed or pasted element will appear.
Clicking in the middle of a word with the I-beam Pointer places the Insertion Point there.

TEXT BASICS

The main difference between a word processing computer and a typewriter is not the way you write, but rather the way you edit and format what you write. You can delete text, replace it, insert more, and change its font and size.

While ruler controls act on paragraphs, the Delete key and the **Font**, **Size** and **Style** menus act on a selection of any length, from a single character to a whole document.

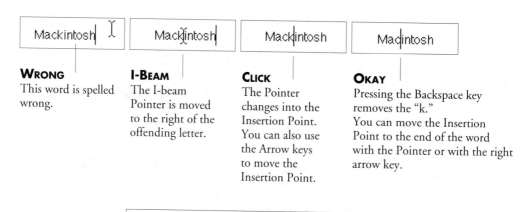

WRONG
This word is spelled wrong.

I-BEAM
The I-beam Pointer is moved to the right of the offending letter.

CLICK
The Pointer changes into the Insertion Point. You can also use the Arrow keys to move the Insertion Point.

OKAY
Pressing the Backspace key removes the "k."
You can move the Insertion Point to the end of the word with the Pointer or with the right arrow key.

Spring is coming, and you all know what this means: we'll have our annual cherry blossom picnic in Ueno Park next week.

SELECT

Format changes apply either to whatever text will be written following the Insertion Point, or to whatever text has been "selected" and appears inverted (white on dark background).

For example, the selected text above could be changed to Italic or to another font.

If "Hanami" (which means cherry blossom viewing, a familiar word to anybody living in Japan) is typed while the text is selected, it replaces the text.

Select a short text by positioning the I-beam Pointer at either end and dragging. A single word can be selected by a double-click.
To select a longer text, click at one end, then go to the other end and Shift-click.

The default font in ClarisWorks is 12-point Helvetica. Some fonts, like Helvetica and Times, are installed on all Macintosh computers. Other fonts are sold by publishers like Adobe.

Fonts with city names (Geneva, New York, etc.) look good on the screen and print well on the ImageWriter dot-matrix printer. You should avoid them if you want to print text on any other printer (LaserWriter, or professional imagesetter).

BIG

Mixing a big letter with small ones increases line spacing throughout the paragraph. While in most word processing programs you can avoid this problem by measuring line spacing in points, in ClarisWorks the line with the big letter then behaves erratically.

You can create nice drop caps (big letters at the beginning of paragraphs), however, by creating a Text *Frame* and using the *Text Wrap* feature (see p. 66)—or by working in Draw mode (see p. 136).

This big letter is called a drop cap.

CONDENSE

Letters that stay nicely together in size 12 tend to come slightly apart in bigger sizes (here, size 48). **Condensed** style may then be used to make a headline stronger.

You can also try to check *fractional character width* in the Preferences dialog box (see p. 30).

Macintosh

Macintosh

TOO MUCH

The style of this word combines Bold, Italic, Outline, Shadow and Underline. Art directors don't recommend this. Here is Greif's rule for Macintosh aesthetics: "That it *can* be done doesn't mean that it *should* be done." ClarisWorks lets you create a headline in Drawing mode and draw a line under it, which looks much better than underlining in Text mode.

SUBSCRIPT/SUPERSCRIPT

H, O and m are size 14 Helvetica.
Number 2 is written in the same size, then selected.
The **Subscript** or **Superscript** command of the **Style** menu is chosen and the size is reduced to 12.

$H_2O \quad m^2$

TEXT BASICS

The paragraph where the Insertion Point blinks is called the "active" paragraph. Changes made on the ruler or in the *Paragraph* dialog box affect either the active paragraph and whatever paragraphs you'll write after it (until you change the ruler again), or several paragraphs which you have selected together.

INDENTS
Dragging the triangle creates a left indent, i.e. a special left margin for the active paragraph or selected paragraphs. Dragging the upside-down "T" creates a first-line indent. See opposite page.

LINE SPACING
Clicking the left or right part of this icon increases or decreases line spacing: half a line if the unit is lines, 1 pt if it is points, etc.

Double-clicking this icon displays the **Paragraph...** dialog box. See opposite page.

COLUMNS
These buttons let you decrease or increase the number of columns.

RIGHT INDENT
Dragging the triangle creates a right indent, i.e. a special right margin for the active paragraph or selected paragraphs.

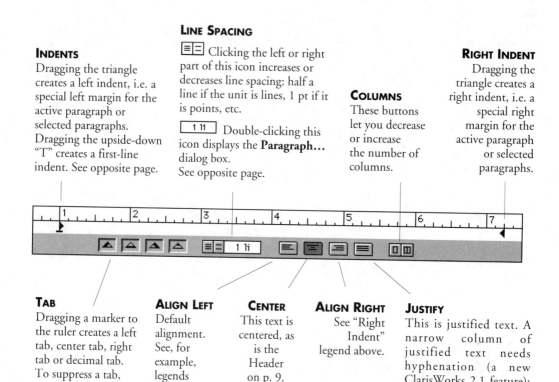

TAB
Dragging a marker to the ruler creates a left tab, center tab, right tab or decimal tab. To suppress a tab, drag the marker off the ruler. See p. 14.

ALIGN LEFT
Default alignment. See, for example, legends throughout this book.

CENTER
This text is centered, as is the Header on p. 9.

ALIGN RIGHT
See "Right Indent" legend above.

JUSTIFY
This is justified text. A narrow column of justified text needs hyphenation (a new ClarisWorks 2.1 feature); otherwise it is easily marred by horrible white gaps. See p. 32.

This is justified text. A narrow column of justified text needs hyphenation (a new ClarisWorks 2.1 feature); otherwise it is easily marred by horrible white gaps.

The left-indent triangle and the first-line-indent upside-down-T have a strange relationship: you can drag the T by itself, but when you drag the triangle, the T follows it; to move the triangle alone, you must press the Option key and drag.

Indents and line spacing can be defined very precisely in the *Paragraph* dialog box, which you display either by choosing the **Paragraph...** command in the **Format** menu or by double-clicking an Alignment button on the ruler.

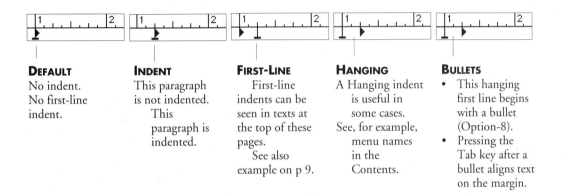

DEFAULT
No indent.
No first-line indent.

INDENT
This paragraph is not indented. This paragraph is indented.

FIRST-LINE
First-line indents can be seen in texts at the top of these pages.
See also example on p 9.

HANGING
A Hanging indent is useful in some cases. See, for example, menu names in the Contents.

BULLETS
• This hanging first line begins with a bullet (Option-8).
• Pressing the Tab key after a bullet aligns text on the margin.

INDENTS

To get the Hanging indent in the example above, you should enter 0.25 inch as Left indent and -0.25 inch as First line indent. Note that other word processors (and common sense) count the Right indent from the right margin: 0 inch instead of 6.25 inch.

SPACING

The little pop-up menus let you choose a unit: line, point, inch, millimeter, centimeter or pica. Points are the usual unit for line spacing (a.k.a. *leading*).

The line spacing for these little legends is 11 pt. This paragraph is separated from the preceding one by an additional 6 pt *Space before*.

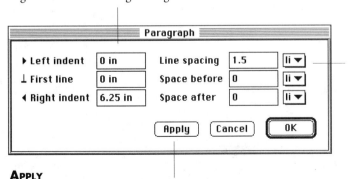

APPLY

This very useful button lets you test several series of numbers until you are satisfied with the look of the paragraph.

TEXT BASICS

Two ways to create a new Tab stop:

1) Drag a triangular Tab marker to the ruler.

2) Display the Tab dialog box by choosing the **Tab...** command in the **Format** menu or by double-clicking the Tab buttons in the gray zone under the ruler.

Two ways to modify an existing Tab stop:

1) Drag it along the ruler.

2) Double-click it to display the Tab dialog box showing its type, fill and position.

DEFAULT

Default invisible Tab stops are located every 0.5 inch. Whenever you create a new Tab stop, it suppresses the default Tab stops at its left.

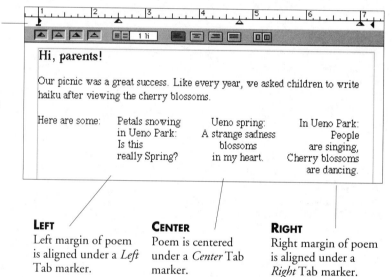

LEFT

Left margin of poem is aligned under a *Left* Tab marker.

CENTER

Poem is centered under a *Center* Tab marker.

RIGHT

Right margin of poem is aligned under a *Right* Tab marker.

DECIMAL

"Align On" applies to a decimal Tab marker.

It lets you replace the default decimal point by a = sign or any other character.

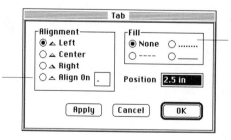

FILL

Here is an example with *Fill:*

Meet at Ueno park 10.00
Speech by Arai san.................12
Lunch....................................12.30
Songs......................................3.00
End 4.30

This is also an example for decimal points aligned under a decimal Tab marker.

In real life, invisible things can't be seen. That's probably why ClarisWorks calls these special symbols, which can be displayed or hidden, *Formatting characters* rather than *Invisible characters* like other programs.

You can be a carefree beginner for a long time without ever needing these characters, but they do prove useful in situations like the example below.

Or let's say something strange happens to your text: it moves suddenly to the next page. By displaying the invisible characters, you may discover that you pressed the Enter key by mistake, thus creating a "Page Break" (see p. 37).

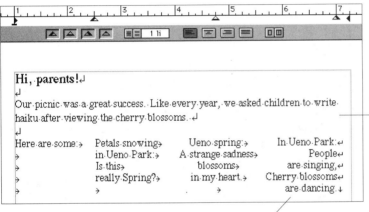

FIVE INVISIBLE GUYS

A dot for a Space,
a small right-pointing arrow for a Tab,
a big bent arrow for a paragraph (return, also called hard return),
a small bent arrow for a line break (soft return),
and a down-pointing arrow for a column or page break.

SOFT RETURN

You create a soft return by simultaneously pressing Shift and Return. Inserting soft returns rather than hard ones at the end of the haiku lines means that the lines are part of the same paragraph. Thus, when the Insertion Point is anywhere in the paragraph that contains all the haiku, moving a tab stop horizontally on the ruler moves the entire haiku. There are many other situations that require soft returns. You'll certainly find them by yourself!

SHORTCUTS

Instead of a **Show/Hide Invisibles** command, ClarisWorks offers an option in the *Preferences* dialog box (see p. 30). Happily, there are two simple shortcuts:
1) The leftmost button on the second line of the Shortcut palette. See more about this palette on p. 21.
2) A keyboard shortcut: ⌘-; (semi-colon).

TEXT MENUS

Text menus are common to all ClarisWorks modes. They let you access basic ClarisWorks features as well as special text ones.

When ClarisWorks is active, two commands are added to the **Apple** menu: **About ClarisWorks...** and **Help....** If the Help file is not installed, choosing **Help...** displays a dialog box asking where Help is located.

You can customize the **Apple** menu by dragging files to the *Apple Menu* folder inside the System folder. You might add "Stationery" files (see p. 21) for the different modes of ClarisWorks to the Apple menu in this way.

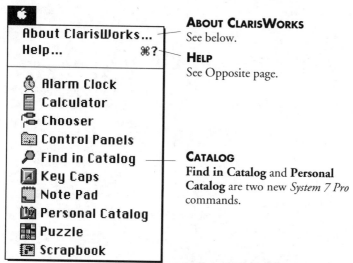

ABOUT CLARISWORKS
See below.

HELP
See Opposite page.

CATALOG
Find in Catalog and **Personal Catalog** are two new *System 7 Pro* commands.

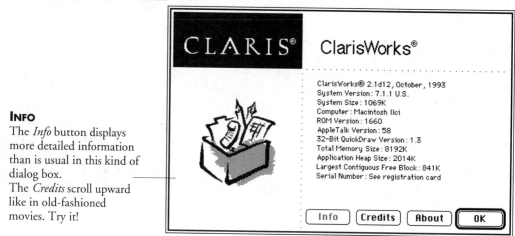

INFO
The *Info* button displays more detailed information than is usual in this kind of dialog box.
The *Credits* scroll upward like in old-fashioned movies. Try it!

The ClarisWorks Help program is a separate HyperCard-type stack of more than two hundred cards which you can leave open behind your ClarisWorks window while you work. The Help program is convenient because it has an interactive "click-and-display" table of contents and index cards, but it is rather tedious, as most cards resemble the one below: no pictures.

NAVIGATION Sends you to cards that explain the mechanics of the Help program.

INDEX Displays an electronic index of ClarisWorks keywords.

RETRACE Returns to the last viewed card, then to the one before that, etc.

PREVIOUS Takes you to the previous card. Shortcut: left keyboard arrow.

NEXT Takes you to the next card. Shortcut: right keyboard arrow.

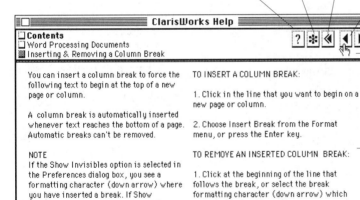

HAND A HyperCard-type *click-once* pointer.

COPY INFO Pressing the Option key changes the hand into an I-beam pointer. You can select text, copy it, then paste it into a ClarisWorks text document or frame. Pressing the Command key changes the pointer into a cross that lets you select and copy text or graphics *as pictures.*

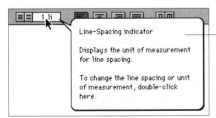

BALLOON System 7 balloons, accessed through the **Show Balloons** command of the **Help** menu (the menu under the question mark at the right of the menu bar) work nicely within ClarisWorks.

The **File** menu, a universal Macintosh menu which lets you create, open, save and print documents, is common to all the ClarisWorks modes. You should definitely know the ⌘-**S** shortcut, and use it often: what you haven't saved is lost if a power shortage or some other mishap occurs. You might as well learn the ⌘-**N**, **O**, **P** and **Q** shortcuts, which exist throughout the Macintosh world.

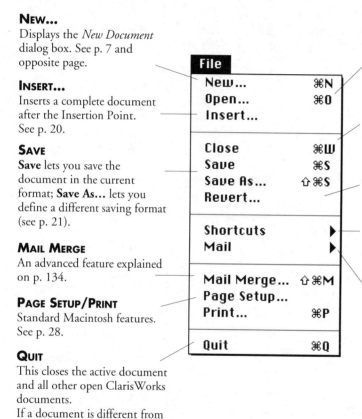

NEW...

Displays the *New Document* dialog box. See p. 7 and opposite page.

INSERT...

Inserts a complete document after the Insertion Point. See p. 20.

SAVE

Save lets you save the document in the current format; **Save As...** lets you define a different saving format (see p. 21).

MAIL MERGE

An advanced feature explained on p. 134.

PAGE SETUP/PRINT

Standard Macintosh features. See p. 28.

QUIT

This closes the active document and all other open ClarisWorks documents.
If a document is different from the version saved on the hard disk, you are asked whether you want to save the changes. Then the ClarisWorks application is closed.

OPEN...

You can open as many documents as memory allows. See p. 20.

CLOSE

Closes the active document, but doesn't close ClarisWorks.

REVERT

Replaces the active document by the version saved on the hard disk. A radical way to undo recent mistakes.

SHORTCUTS AND MACROS

See first submenu below and p. 22.

MAIL

This command is available only if you have System 7 Pro. See second submenu below and p. 26.

New documents are called *Untitled 1*, *Untitled 2*, etc. A traditional Macintosh notation, but a bit of a misnomer. Even if you write a *title* a the top of your page, the document is called *Untitled* as long as you haven't saved and named it. Thus, a better notation for a new document would be *Unnamed 1* or *Unsaved 1*.

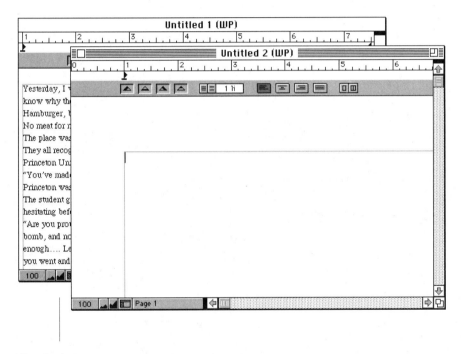

OH GOSH!

It seems that someone has written a lot of stuff in the first document *without saving it*. If a power shortage occurs, or a mysterious bug freezes the screen, all this text will be lost forever.

To avoid such a disaster, you should save and name an important document as soon as you create it, then save it again on a regular basis: every five minutes, say, or whenever you come to the bottom of a page.

Human nature is such that people need to lose twenty or thirty pages of hard work before they acquire the saving reflex!

When several ClarisWorks documents are open at the same time, it's easy to copy elements from one document to another —e.g., to copy a table or graph from a Spreadsheet document to a Text document.

You can also open a non-ClarisWorks document if its format is recognized by a *Claris translator* installed on your Macintosh.

The *Insert* dialog box is similar, but the selected document is imported whole into the active ClarisWorks file rather than opened beside it.

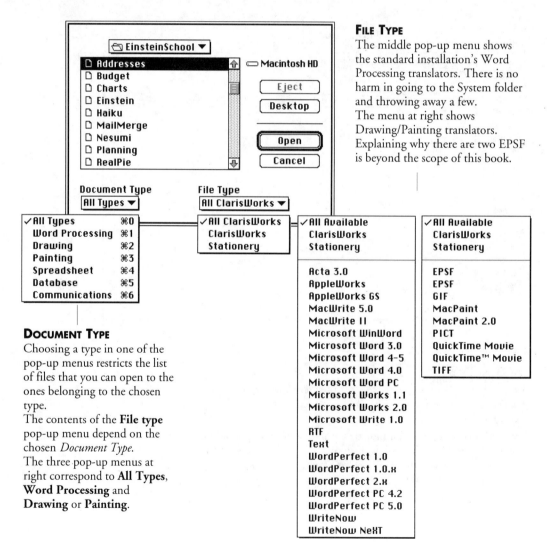

FILE TYPE

The middle pop-up menu shows the standard installation's Word Processing translators. There is no harm in going to the System folder and throwing away a few.

The menu at right shows Drawing/Painting translators. Explaining why there are two EPSF is beyond the scope of this book.

DOCUMENT TYPE

Choosing a type in one of the pop-up menus restricts the list of files that you can open to the ones belonging to the chosen type.

The contents of the **File type** pop-up menu depend on the chosen *Document Type*.

The three pop-up menus at right correspond to **All Types**, **Word Processing** and **Drawing** or **Painting**.

ClarisWorks also gives you a choice of formats when you save a document. For example, if your text were to be read and edited by someone who used Microsoft Word 4 (or 5), you would save a copy under the Microsoft Word 4 format.

You can save a document as *Stationery.* See below.

FOLDER

This folder is where the document will be saved. Clicking its name opens a pop-up menu that shows the hierarchy of folders which contain it; you can "navigate" through the hierarchy by choosing a name in the pop-up menu.

VOLUME

The folder belongs to the *Macintosh HD* hard disk. Clicking this icon lets you climb up the folder hierarchy one step at a time.

DESKTOP

When you click this button, the list of available volumes appears in the main box.

If a floppy disk is inserted inside the drive, its name is included in the list and can be chosen. The document will then be saved onto the floppy disk. This is one of the ways a *backup copy* of the document can be made. No important document should ever exist without a backup copy (or two—some say three).

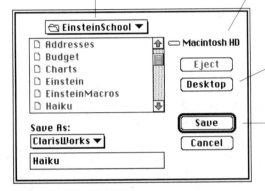

SAVE

This dialog box appears when you choose **Save as...**:
1) To name a document the first time you save it.
2) To save a document under another name or onto another volume.

STATIONERY

Stationery may contain whatever you wish and is often used as a template; you open it to create a new document instead of double-clicking the ClarisWorks icon or choosing the **New...** command. For example, your template might be an empty document with Helvetica replaced by Times as the default font.

Every time you open a Stationery file, it behaves like a new document: it remains "untitled" until you save it for the first time and name it.

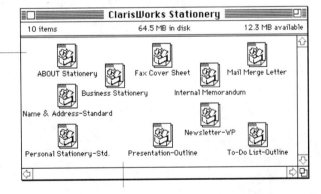

CLARISWORKS STATIONERY

These Stationery files (notice the special icon) are installed in the Claris folder inside the System folder and appear on the pop-up menu of the *New* dialog box (see p. 7).

TEXT MENUS

As computer programs often change, they are prone to sudden fads. Palettes with tiny buttons (called *tools* in Excel) are a current fashion.

While ClarisWorks tools and objects must stay inside a ClarisWorks window, palettes can go anywhere. This is very convenient if you have a big screen: just drag the Shortcuts palette out of the way.

SHOW & EDIT SHORTCUTS

Choose **Show Shortcuts** to display a Shortcuts palette like the one below. Each document type has its own mix of default shortcuts.

To add or remove shortcuts, choose **Edit Shortcuts...**
The size of the palette and the way it "grows" are defined in *Preferences* (see opposite page).

TEXT SHORTCUTS

Default text shortcuts.
Top row: Open, Save, Print, Undo, Cut, Copy, Paste, Bold, Italic, Underline.
Bottom row: Show/Hide Invisibles, Create a Table, Create a Character Style, Copy Ruler, Paste ruler, Increase and Decrease Font Size, Align Left, Align Center and Align Right.

COLLAPSE

The palette collapses to its title bar or expands when you click this box.

EDIT SHORTCUTS

When you click a button in the *Available* or *Installed* box, a short description appears. You can *add* an available shortcut to the collection of installed ones for the active document by checking the *Document* button or for all documents by checking the *Application* button.
You can *remove* an installed shortcut from the palette; it remains available, of course, but is no longer displayed.

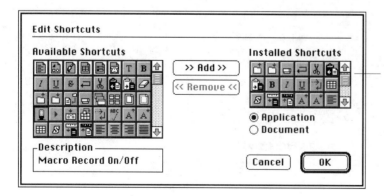

The default Text Shortcuts palette has two rows containing ten buttons each. When you add shortcuts, it "grows" vertically: a third row appears to accomodate more buttons.

The number of buttons on a row and the way the palette grows is defined in the Preferences dialog box (see p. 30).

For a complete list of shortcuts, see Appendix, p. 146.

PALETTE PREFERENCES

Choose **Preferences...** in the **Edit** menu (see p. 30), then click the *Palettes* icon at left to display these options.

See p. 54 for Color palettes.

Grow Limit means *Width* when the palette grows vertically, *Height* when it grows horizontally.

By default, the Shortcuts Palette is not displayed when you open a document. You can decide otherwise here.

If you have a hard time remembering what the button icons stand for, try replacing them with the *Names* of the shortcuts.

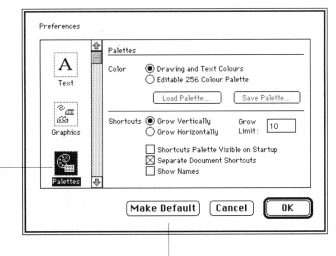

DEFAULT

If you want the options checked here to be true for all ClarisWorks documents, click *Make Default*.

GROW

This palette grows *vertically* with a *Grow limit* of 3 buttons. The bottom row shows three *Separate Document Shortcuts*.

CUSTOM PALETTE

This author prefers to Open/Save/Print/Cut/Paste etc. with keyboard shortcuts, so the corresponding buttons have been removed from this palette.

Three buttons have been added for the Application: Record Macro/Stop Recording, Play Macro, Check Spelling.

Three more buttons are installed on the bottom row for the active document only: Fully Justified Alignment, Superscript and Subscript.

You can also create *custom icons* for macros. See next page.

To create a "macro" is to teach the computer a certain set of tasks that it will then perform automatically when you press a combination of keys or click a button.

This is an important time-saving technique in Spreadsheet and Database mode, but there is no rule against using it for text, as in the example below.

EDIT
Same dialog box as *Record Macro*, with the addition of a pop-up menu showing the list of existing macros. Choosing a macro in the list lets you change its name and features.

PLAY
See opposite page.

DELETE
Same dialog box as *Play Macro*, with a *Delete* button.

Record Macro...	⇧⌘J
Play Macro...	
Edit Macros...	
Delete Macros...	
Macro Wait...	

MACRO WAIT...
This is used only for Communication macros.

RECORD
Try this:
Open a text document. Choose **Record Macro...** to display this dialog box. Enter a letter (for example: h) into the *Option+⌘+Key* box, and a word (for example: Address) into the *Name* box. Click *Record*.
Type the address, "Hasegawa Bldg., 5-3 Maruyama-cho, Shibuya-ku, Tokyo 150 Japan, 03-3780-6641."
Choose the **Stop Recording** command (which replaces **Record macro...** in the submenu) or click the mike button on the palette. That's all.
Now, when the Option, Command and h keys are pressed, the whole address is written magically after the Insertion Point. Note that Macro keyboard shortcuts are case-sensitive: h and H are different.

OPTIONS
The whole idea is that the program records your actions. If you pause because you hesitate, there is no sense in recording and later playing your pause. Check the *Has Shortcut* box to give the macro a shortcut button. Click the gray button at right to edit it (see opposite page).

Record Macro

Name `Untitled 1`

○ Function Key
● Option + ⌘ + Key

Options
☐ Play Pauses
☐ Document Specific
☐ Has Shortcut
☐ In Shortcuts Palette

Play In
☐ All Environments
☒ Word Processing
☐ Drawing
☐ Painting
☒ Database
☐ Spreadsheet
☐ Communications

[Cancel] [Record]

The **Play Macro...** command displays the dialog box below. Since macros are supposed to save time, it seems preferable to play them by using their keyboard or palette shortcut—unless you have created many macros and can't remember their shortcuts.

To display the Button Icon editor, click the blank button in the *Options* box of the Record/Edit Macro dialog box (see opposite page) or Option-click a macro button on a palette.

PLAY

The *Address* macro appears with its custom button.
The *Addit* macro is not available because it is a Spreadsheet macro and the active document is a Text file.
Address is available only for Text and Database.

EDIT BUTTON ICON

Clicking a pixel at left applies to it the color chosen at right.
Creating a picture this way can be a lengthy and even painful process.
It is much easier to create the picture in the Painting module, copy it, and choose the **Paste** command when this dialog box is displayed.
The picture should be small enough—otherwise the program shrinks it in strange ways.
Note that you can't edit an original ClarisWorks button.

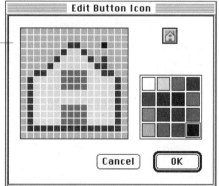

MACRO BUTTON

The new button appears on the palette if the *In Shortcuts Palette* option of the *Record Macro* dialog box is checked.

SHORTCUTS FOR MENU COMMANDS

One use for macros is to create keyboard/button shortcuts for menu commands that lack them. For example, the two buttons at bottom right with tiny arrows stand for macros that choose the **Condense** and **Extend** commands—which have also been given keyboard shortcuts: ⌥-⌘-**C** and **E**.

25

TEXT MENUS

The new ClarisWorks 2.1 *Mail* feature is available only if a particular version of the Macintosh System, called System 7 Pro, is installed on your computer.

You can send mail to other Macs on a network if they also have System 7 Pro—even if they don't have ClarisWorks 2.1.

You can send mail over phone lines to a remote System 7 Pro Macintosh if you have a modem and a program called *PowerTalk Direct Dialup Mail.*

If System 7 Pro is installed on your Mac but not elsewhere on the network, you can still test the feature by sending mail to yourself, as in the example below.

SYSTEM 7 PRO

If System 7 Pro is installed on your Macintosh, you should see these icons on your Desktop.

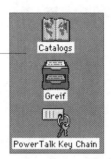

ADD MAILER

Choosing this command adds a top called a *Mailer* to the active document, which becomes a *Letter.* The command then becomes **Remove Mailer**.

SEND

This command is available when the document has a Mailer. See opposite page.

REPLY, FORWARD

These commands are available when you open incoming mail.

MAILER

By default, the sender is the Macintosh "owner" as defined on the network. Clicking the *From* button lets you change the sender's name—if you know a registered *Key Chain* password.

You can drag an *Information card* from the Desktop to the *Recipients* box or click the Recipients button to display an *Address Panel* that lets you look for recipients.

Mail cannot be sent without a *Subject,* which you type inside the *Subject* box.

You can send *Enclosures*—up to fifty files or folders—with your letter. Clicking the *Enclosures* button displays an Open-type dialog box.

A little paper-clip icon at the top right of the Mailer signals that the Letter has enclosures.

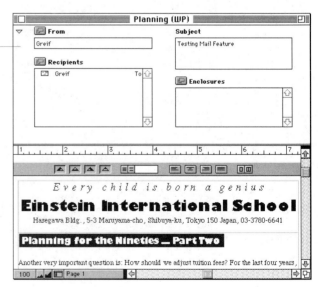

Here is a complete send-and-receive sequence. Consult your System 7 Pro manual for more info.

SENDING

Choosing the **Send...** command opens this dialog box. The pop-up menu gives you a choice of formats: ClarisWorks, AppleMail, Snapshot (the letter as picture), plus all the formats of the *Save* dialog box.

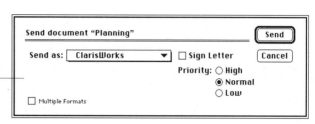

RECEIVING

A beep and an alert box have warned Greif that mail just arrived. Opening the Desktop Mailbox shows one letter from Greif inside the *In Tray*. *Priority* is just a label: it doesn't affect transmission speed.

OPENING THE LETTER

A double-click on the Letter icon in the *In Tray* opens the letter. Notice that here the Mailer is *collapsed*. The tiny triangle at left lets you collapse/expand it.

REPLYING

When you choose the **Reply** command, the program opens a new Untitled document. By default, it contains the original letter in Italic style —without its Header.

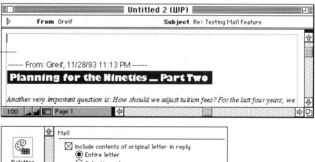

MAIL PREFERENCES

Default choices are shown here. You might try to *Show options when closing a letter:* this lets you "tag" the letter, a useful feature if you want to organize your mail. See your System 7 Pro manual about this.

TEXT MENUS

The standard Macintosh dialog boxes shown on these two pages offer options for most LaserWriter and StyleWriter printers. Other printers may have slightly different options. Consult your printer's manual.

If your document does not include bitmap text (i.e., pre-TrueType Chicago) and Paint mode pictures, you can just accept these default settings—and go directly to the opposite page.

PRINTER EFFECTS
Font Substitution and *Text Smoothing* affect pre-TrueType versions of fonts with city names (e.g., Geneva or New York). You might as well avoid these fonts altogether, as substitution often modifies spacing and alignment.
Graphics Smoothing smoothes Paint-type pictures. Turn it off if you want a sharp rendering of fine details, especially if they are inverted (white on a dark background).
Nobody knows what *Faster Bitmap Printing* does.

PAPER
US Letter: 8.5 " x 11 "
A4 Letter: 8.25 " x 11.66 "
US Legal: 8.5 " x 14 "
B5 Letter: 8.25 " x 12 "
The *Tabloid* pop-up menus offers more special sizes.

REDUCE/ENLARGE
From 25% to 400% (on a regular LaserWriter).

ORIENTATION
Printing sideways is the sensible choice for some Spreadsheet or Draw/Paint documents.

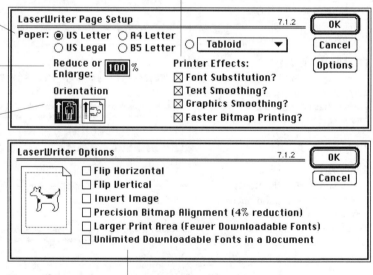

OPTIONS
The *Options* button opens this dialog box.
Try *Flip Horizontal, Flip Vertical, Invert Image,* and see what happens to the little dog (seen by some people as a cow).
Precision Bitmap Alignment is a must if you print unsmoothed Paint pictures.
Larger Print Area means a 0.25 inch margin instead of 0.5.
Downloadable Fonts are fonts like Garamond, which are not permanent residents of the LaserWriter's memory and are *downloaded* each time they are printed.

ClarisWorks Text documents are *wysiwyg* (what you see is what you get). Thus, if you check a Text document on screen very carefully before printing, you should not be surprised by the printer's output.

For other types, you need to choose **Page View** in the **View** menu to see how the program will print the document.

TAB

In dialog boxes, pressing the Tab key sends the Insertion Point from one little box to the next one. For example, to print from p. 1 to p. 5, you would press Tab, type 1, press Tab, type 5, then press Return or Enter as a shortcut for clicking the *Print* button.

FROM

To print only p. 5, you should enter From: 5 To: 5.

COVER

A special page with the document's name, printing time, and other info, to be printed before or after the document.

```
LaserWriter  "Personal LaserWriter NT"          7.1.2      [ Print ]
Copies: [1]        Pages: ● All ○ From: [   ] To: [   ]    [ Cancel ]
Cover Page:   ● No ○ First Page ○ Last Page
Paper Source: ● Paper Cassette ○ Manual Feed
Print:        ● Black & White ○ Color/Grayscale
Destination:  ● Printer        ○ PostScript® File
```

COLOR/GRAYSCALE

Some printers render grayscale pictures very nicely, but when printing proofs, you save a lot of time by choosing Black & White.

POSTSCRIPT FILE

Check this option if you are sending a document to a Service bureau for printing—and the Service bureau requests it.

SPREADSHEET

These options appear at the bottom of the dialog box when the document is a Spreadsheet.

```
⊠ Print Column Headings   ⊠ Print Row Headings
⊠ Print Cell Grid
```

```
Print:        ○ Current Record  ● Visible Records
```

DATABASE

This option appears at the bottom of the dialog box when the document belongs to the Database mode.

29

TEXT MENUS

While the **File** menu doesn't change at all from one mode of ClarisWorks to another, the **Insert Date/Time/Page #** part of the **Edit** menu is specific to the Text mode, and is replaced by other commands in other modes.

The first six commands of this menu exist in most Macintosh programs. Learning their keyboard shortcuts saves a lot of time.

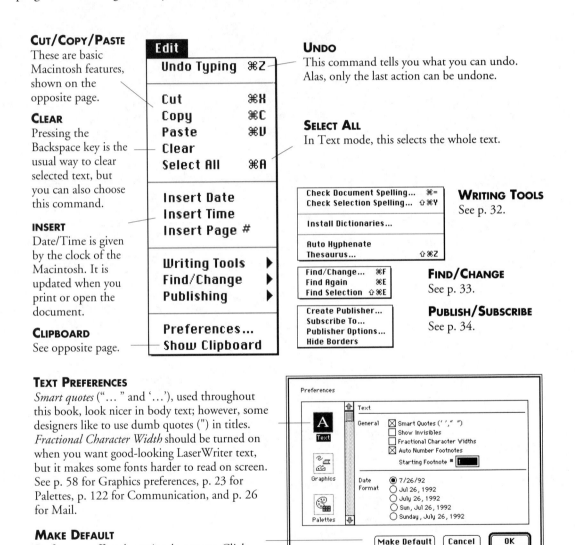

CUT/COPY/PASTE
These are basic Macintosh features, shown on the opposite page.

CLEAR
Pressing the Backspace key is the usual way to clear selected text, but you can also choose this command.

INSERT
Date/Time is given by the clock of the Macintosh. It is updated when you print or open the document.

CLIPBOARD
See opposite page.

UNDO
This command tells you what you can undo. Alas, only the last action can be undone.

SELECT ALL
In Text mode, this selects the whole text.

WRITING TOOLS
See p. 32.

FIND/CHANGE
See p. 33.

PUBLISH/SUBSCRIBE
See p. 34.

TEXT PREFERENCES
Smart quotes ("…" and '…'), used throughout this book, look nicer in body text; however, some designers like to use dumb quotes (") in titles. *Fractional Character Width* should be turned on when you want good-looking LaserWriter text, but it makes some fonts harder to read on screen. See p. 58 for Graphics preferences, p. 23 for Palettes, p. 122 for Communication, and p. 26 for Mail.

MAKE DEFAULT
Preferences affect the active document. Click here if you want them for all new documents.

30

Edit: Cut/Copy and Paste

In the pictures below, **A** represents an element of text: a letter, a word, a paragraph, or several pages. **B** and **C** represent more text. In word processing, the Cut and Paste feature is often used to move an element of text elsewhere. In this example, **A** is moved between **B** and **C**.

Elements of text, graphic objects, etc. can be cut/copied and pasted from one document to another. You can also paste elements that you want to keep handy into the **Scrapbook** (in the **Apple** menu).

SELECT
Text **A** is selected. See how to select text on p. 10.

CUT
The **Cut** command is chosen.
Text **A** seems to disappear, but it is saved inside a special memory called the Clipboard (where it replaces whatever was cut or copied before).
If you worry easily, you can keep track of **A** by choosing the **Show Clipboard** command, which displays the window below.

MOVE INSERTION POINT
The Insertion Point is moved between text **B** and text **C**.

PASTE
When the **Paste** command is chosen, text **A** appears between text **B** and text **C**.
It stays in the Clipboard and can thus be pasted several times in different places.
If **A** was copied rather than cut, the sequence would be: **ABC**, **A|BC**, **AB|C**, **ABAC**.
If you want to be absolutely sure that **A** won't be lost between **Cut** and **Paste** due to a power failure or something, go the **Copy** way, then delete the old **A**: **ABC**, **A|BC**, **AB|C**, **ABAC**, **BAC**.

FORMAT
Cut or copied text keeps its character and paragraph formats when pasted inside ClarisWorks, but may lose them when pasted into another program.

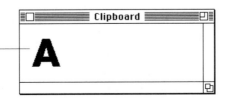

ClarisWorks lacks the wonderful check-spelling-as-you-type feature common to other Claris programs.

When you check a text, keep the pointer over the *Skip* button and be ready to click fast. When checking the letter on p. 9, for example, the program stumbles already on the first line (see *Spelling* dialog box below).

The Thesaurus is a marvelous add-on. Try it!

HYPHENATE

This command hyphenates the whole document. Editing the Hyphenation dictionary lets you add words with custom hyphens or with no hyphens.

To hyphenate a word in a text, type ⌘-Hyphen (*Discretionary hyphen*).

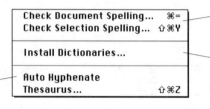

CHECK SPELLING

See below.

INSTALL DICTIONARIES

An Open-type dialog box lets you install regular dictionaries and thesauruses; install and edit Hyphenation dictionaries; and install, create, and edit User dictionaries (See *Learn*, below).

QUESTIONABLE WORD

This is the date on top of the p. 9 letter. The program skipped the Header, which can be checked separately when active.

REPLACE

Replaces questionable word with suggestion or selection.

CHECK

Checks a word that you enter directly into the dialog box.

SKIP

Accepts the word as is.

LEARN

Adds word (e.g., a proper noun) to the *User Dictionary*.

FLAG

Displays the word's context.

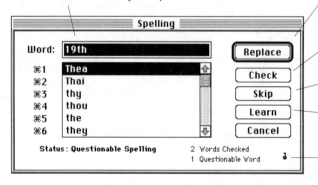

THESAURUS

The word *Sadness* (in the second haiku) is selected. *Sorrow* is one of the synonyms. Selecting it, then clicking *Lookup*, displays the list at right. *Bale* is next!

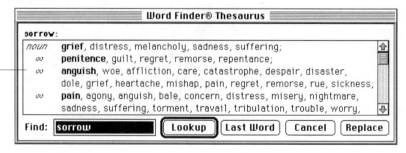

Edit: Spelling, Find

Finding an element of text, and replacing it with another, is one task where computers really outshine human beings.

This feature may be used to replace unwanted double-spaces between words by single spaces: click inside the *Find* box and press the Space bar twice, then press the Space bar once inside the *Change* box.

You can search for invisible characters. To find Return, Tab, or Enter (column/page break), press ⌘-Return, Tab, or Enter or enter \p (for Paragraph), \t or \c. The code for soft return is \n; codes for automatic date, time, and page number are \d, \h, and \#. The code for \ is \\.

FIND/CHANGE
This displays the dialog box below.

FIND SELECTION
Finds the next occurence of a selected element of text.

FIND AGAIN
A just-found word stays in the dialog box. This looks for its next occurence without opening the dialog box.

WHOLE WORD
When this button is not checked, "Find *Cher*" finds cherry and butcher, etc. When it is checked, it finds only cher or Cher. When Case Sensitive is checked, it finds only Cher.

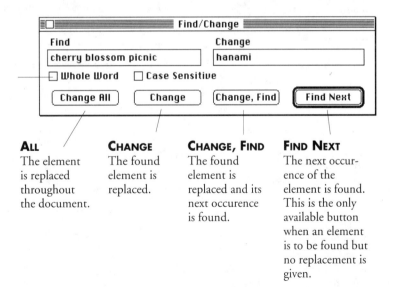

ALL
The element is replaced throughout the document.

CHANGE
The found element is replaced.

CHANGE, FIND
The found element is replaced and its next occurence is found.

FIND NEXT
The next occurence of the element is found. This is the only available button when an element is to be found but no replacement is given.

33

TEXT MENUS

The Publish/Subscribe feature lets you link a source *(Publisher)* to a destination *(Subscriber)*. Then, whenever you modify the Publisher, the Subscriber is changed automatically. The source and destination can belong to different applications supporting this feature (like ClarisWorks and Adobe Illustrator, etc.) and to different Macintosh computers on the same network.

Most applications can't communicate directly, so the linking is done through a special kind of file called an *Edition*.

PUBLISH/SUBSCRIBE
The **Create Publisher...** command is available only when some text (or Draw-type picture or spreadsheet table) is selected. It displays the dialog box below.

> Create Publisher...
> Subscribe To...
> Publisher Options...
> Hide Borders

CREATE PUBLISHER
You can save the Edition wherever you wish—possibly in a Shared Folder on a network.
Preview is also available in the *Subscribe* dialog box, where it lets you verify what you're subscribing to.

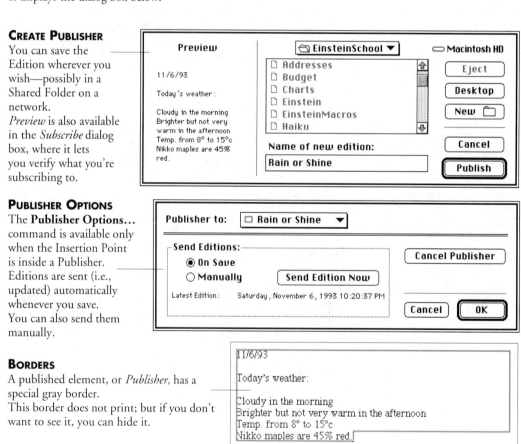

PUBLISHER OPTIONS
The **Publisher Options...** command is available only when the Insertion Point is inside a Publisher. Editions are sent (i.e., updated) automatically whenever you save. You can also send them manually.

BORDERS
A published element, or *Publisher*, has a special gray border.
This border does not print; but if you don't want to see it, you can hide it.

In this example, several classrooms subscribe to the weather report published by a group of pupils. Choosing the **Subscribe to...** command displays a dialog box similar to the *Create Publisher* one, which lists available Editions. When you subscribe to an Edition, the Subscriber appears at the Insertion Point. It has the same gray border as the Publisher.

All this would work just as well if the weather report was a beautiful color map made in the Draw module. You can't, however, publish a Paint picture.

Note that you can publish an element in a document and subscribe to it in the same document—to change all its occurences automatically when you modify the first one.

SUBSCRIBER OPTIONS

When you select the Subscriber, the **Publisher Options...** command is replaced by **Subscriber Options...**
Default update is automatic—whenever the Edition is updated.

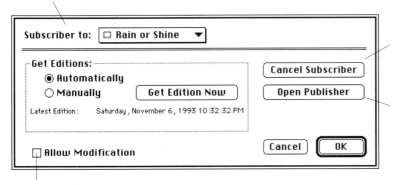

ALLOW MODIFICATION

This option is available for text only. Besides, any change to the Subscriber will be lost when it is updated.

EDITION

An Edition's icon has the same gray border as the Publisher and the Subscriber.
When you double-click such an icon, a little Preview box is displayed. Here, too, opening the Publisher is not always possible.

Rain or Shine

CANCEL SUBSCRIBER

When you cancel, the Subscriber becomes ordinary text or graphics. You can't throw away an Edition unless you have cancelled all its subscribers.

OPEN PUBLISHER

Opening the Publisher to edit it is not always possible. For example, an Edition located on some other Macintosh should belong to a shared folder, so that you can access it, but the Publisher behind the Edition may be out of reach.

TEXT MENUS

The **Format** menu lets you define how your page and its contents look and print.

The **Columns...**, **Insert Break**, and **Insert Footnote** commands are specific to the Text mode **Format** menu.

In Graphics and Database modes, the **Format** menu includes submenus for Font, Size and Style.

COPY RULER

This command copies the attributes of the active paragraph, including not only ruler-defined attributes, but also those chosen in the Paragraph and Tab dialog boxes, e.g. *Space Before, Fill*, etc. These attributes can then be applied to another paragraph (or set of selected paragraphs) by clicking it (or selecting them) and choosing **Apply Ruler**. Notice that the keyboard shortcuts are cousins of the Copy and Paste ones.

HEADER, FOOTER

See p. 9.

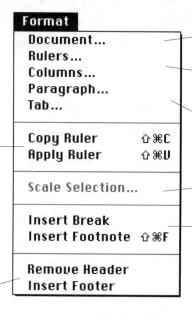

DOCUMENT

See dialog box below.

RULERS, COLUMNS

See opposite page.

PARAGRAPH, TAB

See p. 12 for Paragraph and p. 14 for Tab.

SCALE

This applies only to graphics. See p. 64.

BREAK, FOOTNOTE

See opposite page.
If *Auto Number Footnotes* is not checked in Preferences (see p. 30), the **Insert Footnote** command displays a dialog box asking you for a footnote mark—"*", "†", etc.

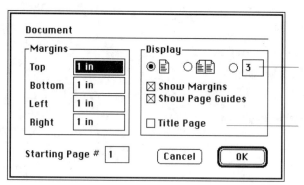

DISPLAY

Here, you can choose a number of pages to be displayed on screen side by side.
You can't have symmetrical page numbers in footers, like those in this book.

TITLE PAGE

When this option is checked, the first page of the document has no header and no footer.

The example below shows two columns. A "break" was inserted after the word Children! (notice the formatting character, a tiny arrow pointing down), so the rest of the text was pushed to the next column. A break in a one-column page pushes the text to the next page.

A footnote was inserted after *Park*. A number appeared after the word in superscript, and its corresponding marker appeared at the bottom of the page, followed by the Insertion Point.

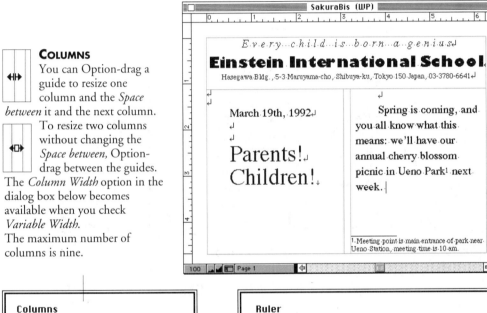

COLUMNS

You can Option-drag a guide to resize one column and the *Space between* it and the next column.

To resize two columns without changing the *Space between*, Option-drag between the guides.

The *Column Width* option in the dialog box below becomes available when you check *Variable Width*.

The maximum number of columns is nine.

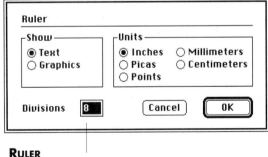

Columns

- ◉ Equal width
- ○ Variable width

Number of **2**

Column width ▼ 3.04 in

Space between 0.17 in

[Cancel] [OK]

Ruler

Show
- ◉ Text
- ○ Graphics

Units
- ◉ Inches ○ Millimeters
- ○ Picas ○ Centimeters
- ○ Points

Divisions **8** [Cancel] [OK]

RULER

By default, Text documents have *Text* rulers (see pp. 9, 12, 14, etc.), but they can have *Graphics* rulers like the example above.

Invisible *Divisions* define the *Grid* (see p. 61).

TEXT MENUS

With the commands in the **Font**, **Size** and **Style** menus, you can alter the appearance of selected text in several ways. When no text is selected, the commands apply to the text you write from the Insertion Point on.

See some examples of styles on p. 11.

Most style commands can be "toggled." For example, choosing **Bold** (or pressing ⌘-**B**) changes a non-bold selection to bold or a bold selection to non-bold. If the text was bold and italic, it becomes italic only. Choosing **Plain Text** removes all the styles.

Font	Size	Style	
Chicago	**9 Point**	✓**Plain Text**	⌘T
Courier	10 Point	**Bold**	⌘B
Geneva	12 Point	*Italic*	⌘I
✓Helvetica	14 Point	<u>Underline</u>	⌘U
Monaco	✓18 Point	~~Strike Thru~~	
New York	24 Point	Outline	
Palatino	36 Point	Shadow	
Σψμβολ	48 Point	Condense	
Times	72 Point	Extend	
		Superscript	⇧⌘+
	Other... ⇧⌘O	Subscript	⇧⌘-
		Text Color ▶	
		Define Styles...	

NO SHORTCUTS
Macros let you give shortcuts to commands that lack them.
See p. 24.

TEXT COLOR
Maximum number of colors for text is 81.

DEFINE STYLES
See opposite page.

FONT AND SIZE
In the **Font** menu, each font name shows how the font looks. Pressing the Option key when opening the menu displays the names in Chicago font as in other menus. There are three kinds of fonts:
1) City-named fonts (don't use them!)
2) TrueType fonts. They look good on screen at whatever size you choose, but do not always print well on a PostScript laser printer.
3) Adobe Type 1 fonts. Outlined numbers in the **Size** menu show sizes that look good on-screen. Other sizes look jagged on screen, but print okay. Non-outlined sizes look good if a program called Adobe Type Manager (ATM) is installed on your Macintosh.
Other Size limits: from 4 pt to 255 pt.

Character Styles let you format elements of text in one shot. In the example below, "Headline" style is Helvetica Bold 24 pt Red and "Subhead" is Times 18 pt Blue. Instead of choosing several commands in several menus to format a headline or a subhead, you just choose the appropriate Character Style.

It would be nice if headlines could be centered as well, but alignment is a paragraph attribute, not a character attribute. Dedicated word processors let you create *Paragraph Styles*. In ClarisWorks, you can simulate paragraph styles with macros. To create a Headline macro: Start recording, choose **Headline** at the bottom of the **Style** menu, click the icon for centered alignment on the ruler, and stop recording.

CUSTOM STYLES

Choosing the **Define Styles...** command displays this dialog box. The font, size, style and color showing inside the dialog box are those of the text at the Insertion Point (or selected text). Thus, you can define a Character Style on your page before opening the dialog box, or you can do so within the dialog box. After you enter a name and click *Add*, the name is added to the list of style names.

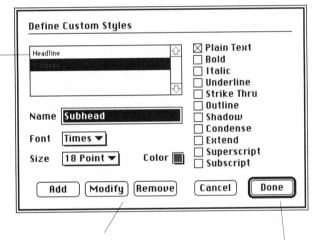

MODIFY, REMOVE

These buttons become available only when a style name is selected in the list. Whereas in Microsoft Word, modifying a style changes all paragraphs with this style, in ClarisWorks styles are forgotten once applied. If you modify the *Headline* style and want all headlines modified, you must select them one by one and apply the new style to them.

DONE

When you click this button, the new or modified styles are saved and appear at the bottom of the **Style** menu. The first nine styles are assigned keyboard shortcuts.

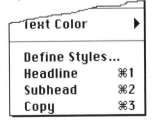

Outline View is a kind of submode inside the Text module that can help you organize your text.

Creating an outline with this feature is easier and more fun than the boring outlines you had to write in college: you can drag topics up or down, change their level of importance, and collapse or expand them. Some people consider outlining programs very powerful tools of creativity.

OUTLINE VIEW
This command lets you toggle between **Outline View** and regular view.

FORMATS, LABELS
Default is Diamond. See other formats and labels on p. 43.

NEW TOPIC
Using these commands is fine, but hitting the Return key is an easier way to create a new topic. You can then move it right or left if you want.
Note that if you have changed the topic's style with the **Font**, **Size** or **Style** menu, ⌘-Return creates a new topic with the original style of its level (i.e., without the changes).

MOVE LEFT, ETC.
See opposite page.
Forget the shortcuts shown on the menu and remember: Control-keyboard arrow.

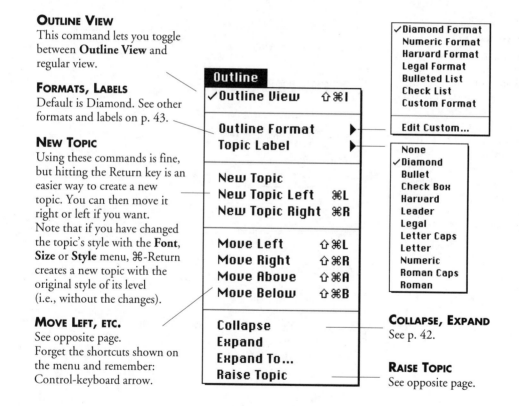

COLLAPSE, EXPAND
See p. 42.

RAISE TOPIC
See opposite page.

One way to use the power of the Outline feature is to simply jot down ideas in regular Text mode, then turn to Outline View to organize them.

Constantly pulling down the menu is tedious, so you should remember the Control-Arrow shortcuts. Microsoft Word has very convenient buttons for outlining commands; if you appreciate outlining and do a lot of it, you might create your own macros and shortcut buttons.

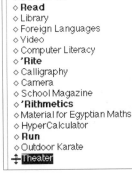

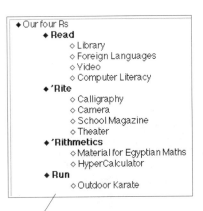

PARAGRAPHS

In Outline View, paragraphs will become *Topics*. Thus, when you jot down your ideas, you should begin a new line (by pressing Return) for each one.

In this example, some items have been manually set to bold—this is not an automatic style.

OUTLINE VIEW

Choosing **Outline View** changes paragraphs into *Topics*. Every topic is marked by a *Topic Label* (by default, diamonds; see also p. 43).

Now you can move topics up and down by dragging their labels. This is just what is happening to *Theatre* above: it will move from sports ("Run") to arts ("'Rite").

LEVELS

At first, all the topics belong to the same *Level* (namely, Level 1).

You move a topic to the right, i.e. demote it to Level 2, by pressing Control-→. It thus becomes a *Subtopic* of the Level 1 topic above it.

A topic with subtopics has a black label.

Clicking a black label selects the topic *and* its subtopics. Now, when you drag a label up or down, the subtopics come with the topic. This is also true when you move the topic left or right.

To move a topic *without* its subtopics, put the Insertion Point inside the topic, then press the Option key before you choose one of the **Move** commands in the menu.

Note two different ways of raising a topic: **Move Left** raises it so that other same-level topics below it become its subtopics; **Raise Topic** moves it below same-level topics first, so that it is raised without getting new subtopics.

When you move topics up, down, right and left a lot because you are trying different ways of expressing your ideas, you do not need to see subtopics. You can be sure that they are following their parents faithfully!

That's why it is possible to *Collapse* a topic, i.e. hide its subtopics and the subtopics of its subtopics.

This feature is especially useful with a long outline. By judicious collapsing, you can display the whole outline on your screen and really move things around.

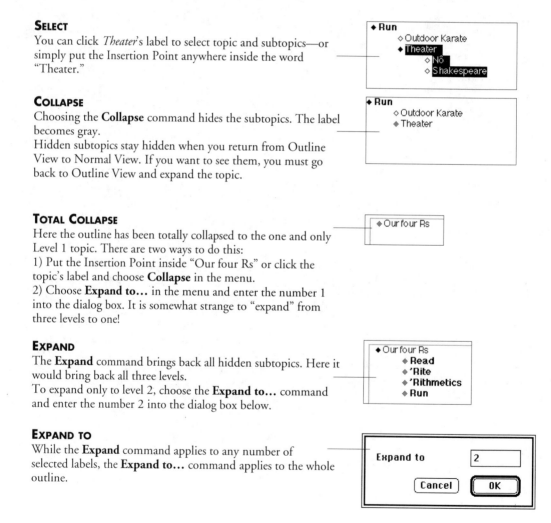

SELECT

You can click *Theater*'s label to select topic and subtopics—or simply put the Insertion Point anywhere inside the word "Theater."

COLLAPSE

Choosing the **Collapse** command hides the subtopics. The label becomes gray.

Hidden subtopics stay hidden when you return from Outline View to Normal View. If you want to see them, you must go back to Outline View and expand the topic.

TOTAL COLLAPSE

Here the outline has been totally collapsed to the one and only Level 1 topic. There are two ways to do this:

1) Put the Insertion Point inside "Our four Rs" or click the topic's label and choose **Collapse** in the menu.

2) Choose **Expand to...** in the menu and enter the number 1 into the dialog box. It is somewhat strange to "expand" from three levels to one!

EXPAND

The **Expand** command brings back all hidden subtopics. Here it would bring back all three levels.

To expand only to level 2, choose the **Expand to...** command and enter the number 2 into the dialog box below.

EXPAND TO

While the **Expand** command applies to any number of selected labels, the **Expand to...** command applies to the whole outline.

Outline: Collapse, Edit

The program offers several preset styles for outlines: numbers; bullets, etc. You can add your own custom format to them (alas, one custom format only). All labels can be clicked to select a topic and dragged up and down—except check boxes, which, when clicked, are checked or unchecked.

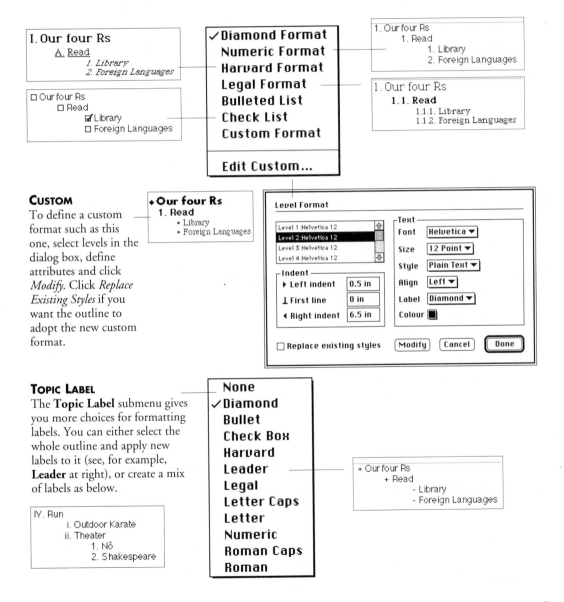

CUSTOM

To define a custom format such as this one, select levels in the dialog box, define attributes and click *Modify.* Click *Replace Existing Styles* if you want the outline to adopt the new custom format.

TOPIC LABEL

The **Topic Label** submenu gives you more choices for formatting labels. You can either select the whole outline and apply new labels to it (see, for example, **Leader** at right), or create a mix of labels as below.

43

The commands in the **View** menu do not change the document itself—only the way it is displayed.

You need different view options to increase useful display space when working with a small screen. Other important view commands do not appear on this menu—see below and opposite page.

NEW VIEW
See p. 47.

PAGE VIEW
This command is not available for Text documents, but only for documents in other modes. When **Page View** is unchecked, Header, Footer and margins are hidden, providing a better view of the document.

TOOLS, RULERS
These commands toggle between **Show** and **Hide**.
In default Text documents, tools are hidden and the ruler is shown. Showing tools is necessary if you want to add drawings or a spreadsheet frame to the document.

HIDE MARGINS
You can hide a Text document's margins—which is what unchecking **Page View** does in other modes—in the *Document* dialog box (see p. 36).
This makes a big difference when you write in earnest. On a small screen, a sentence sitting astride a page break can't be seen whole (see top picture at right) unless you hide the margins (see bottom picture).
As you can't hide Header and Footer for a Text document, it's best to create them at the last moment.

OPEN FRAME
When a table is shown as a spreadsheet "frame" inside another document (see p. 130), you can "open the frame" to see as much of the spreadsheet as the size of the window allows.

SLIDE SHOW
See p. 48.

TILE, STACK WINDOWS
See p. 46.

EINSTEIN
The list of open documents is shown here. You can bring a hidden window to the front by checking its name.

View
New View
Open Frame

✓Page View ⇧⌘P
Slide Show...

Hide Tools ⇧⌘T
Hide Rulers ⇧⌘U

Tile Windows
Stack Windows

Einstein (DR)
✓Untitled 1 (WP)

that.... But she took her Hamburger and moved to another

I really hate it when they say, "your bomb." I wanted to tell her that I had never killed anybody, that the people who should have stayed home were the ones who voted for Hitler in 1933, that.... But she took her Hamburger and moved to another

table. A very young girl she was, with blonde hair and nice round American cheeks.

View: Scale

In version 1.0 of ClarisWorks (for Macintosh or Windows), a **View Scale...** command in the **View** menu displays the *View scale* dialog box. In ClarisWorks 2.0, a pop-up menu appears when you click the scale number and you choose the **Other...** command to display the dialog box.

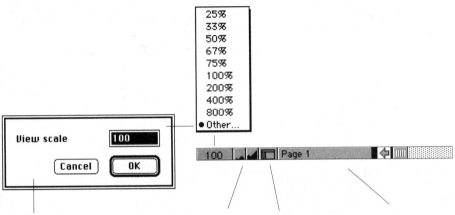

VIEW SCALE
Authorized view scale: any number between 3.125 and 3200. The example below shows how the 11 point Garamond font—used for the body text in this book—looks on screen. Setting the scale to 127 (i.e., 14/11) changes the apparent size to 14 point, which is much easier to read.

MOUNTAINS
Clicking a little mountain button zooms in or out from the page.
When you start from 100, preset scale values are 67, 50, 33, 25, 12.5, 6.25 and 3.125; 200, 400, 800, 1600 and 3200. When you start from a custom scale, the value is halved or doubled.

SHOW/HIDE TOOLS
Clicking this button shows or hides the Tool panel.
This is really much more convenient than choosing the **Show Tools** command in the menu.

GO TO PAGE
A double-click on the Page Indicator displays the *Go to page* dialog box.

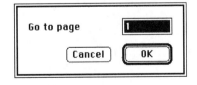

TEXT MENUS

The first picture below shows how the **Tile Windows** command neatly arranges four windows. These can contain four different documents, as here, or different *Views* (see opposite page) of one or more documents.

The second picture shows the top of the windows after the **Stack Windows** command has been chosen.

Both display modes let you activate a window by clicking it. If a window is hidden behind another one, you can tile or stack to see it and activate it, but it is simpler to choose its name at the bottom of the **View** menu.

TILED

Two or three windows are tiled by default as horizontal bands.
If you prefer vertical bands, press Option before you scroll the **View** menu and choose the command.

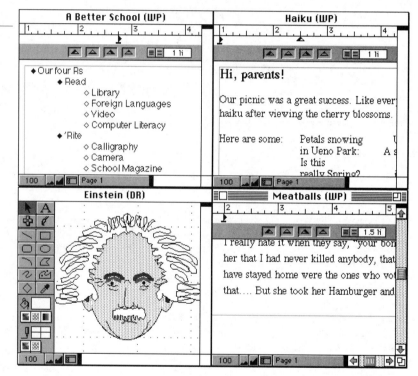

STACKED

The command not only stacks the windows, but puffs them up to the size of the screen.

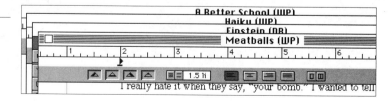

46

View: Tile, Stack, New

The first picture below shows how you can juxtapose several views of the same document inside one window by "splitting" the window into *Panes*. The panes can show distant parts of the document at the same time, but display features such as scale are identical.

In the second picture, there are also two views of the same document, but they belong to different windows. Their scales can be different (and each one can be split). In this database example, one view shows the document in *Browse* mode, the other in *Layout* mode.

SPLITTING A WINDOW

Dragging the small black box ("Pane Tool") at the top of the scroll bar divides the window into two panes. You can then scroll inside each pane to view different pages at the same time.

The other Pane Tool, at the bottom of the window, lets you create vertical panes. A double splitting creates four panes.

Here, you might want to give *Planning for the Nineties* the same font and style as *Our four Rs*. In such a situation, seeing the two together may help.

Dragging the Pane Tool upward suppresses the division.

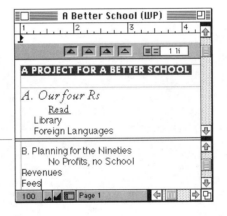

NEW VIEW

The **New View** command creates a new window containing the same document.

This is useful for pictures: you can work at scale 400 or 800 in one window while seeing how the scale 100 picture in the other window is affected.

While splitting a window usually creates two panes, or at most four, the number of New Views is limited only by the computer's memory.

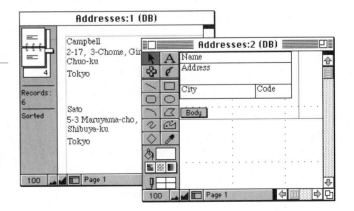

TEXT MENUS

The **Slide Show...** command displays the dialog box shown on the opposite page. As when showing real photo slides, you must create "slides" before you choose the command and start the show. This means preparing a series of ClarisWorks pages with text, pictures, Spreadsheet tables and charts, or Database records. The slide show takes place on the screen—unless you link an electronic projector to the Macintosh.

PICTURE AND TEXT

This picture was created in a Draw mode document. You should see it in color!
There is no law against creating a slide show in Text mode, but Drawing mode is really better adapted for presentations. You can use the *Master Page* feature (see p. 65) to full effect; bring in a series of objects one by one in successive slides; move items; etc. Note that Painting mode is okay for slides if you have a fast computer and lots of memory.
In this example, the text is written inside two slightly offset frames—a black text in front of a red one—on the second page of the document. When the slide show begins, the screen becomes black (the menus are hidden) and the picture appears.
After a few seconds, the second slide, with the text, appears in front of the first one.
As it is "transparent," it does not replace the picture, but simply adds the text to it.

Drawing mode documents usually have one page, so how do you produce all the pages for the slide show? The answer can be seen on p. 60: you can enter any number of pages for a Draw document into the *Document* dialog box. When there are several pages *across* and *down*, the slide show follows a logical order: across and down.

Border

Background

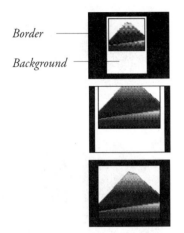

SLIDE OPTIONS

Let's say you've drawn a nice picture that more or less fits the screen. The *Fit to window* option shrinks the picture so that the whole page, including the useless white part under the picture, fits inside the window (first example at left). *Center* does not shrink the picture but crops it (second example). For the slide on the opposite page (and the third example at left), both these options have been unchecked. You *Show cursor* if you want to point items on the slide during the show. *Fade* means *Fade to black*.

If you do not check the Automatic Advance, you can show the next slide by clicking the mouse or by pressing the right arrow or space bar; press the left arrow for the previous slide.

Slides usually look much better when *Background* and *Border* are the same color.

ORDER

You can select a page number and drag it up or down to change the order of the slides.

Clicking the icon at left of the page order changes the mode from *Opaque* to *Transparent* to *Hidden.*

A transparent slide lets you see the preceding one through it. You can add words and objects progressively in this way.

You might hide a page that you don't want to show but need to keep.

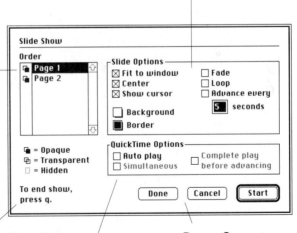

END

Press "q" or Escape to stop the slide show.

QUICKTIME

With *Auto play*, the movie starts as soon as the slide appears.

When several movies are present on the slide, *Simultaneous* starts them all.

Complete play overrides the *Advance every n seconds* timing.

DONE, START

Done saves the options without running the show. You can run the show without displaying the dialog box by pressing Option when you choose **Slide Show…** in the **View** menu.

Draw

Drawing mode pictures are "objects" made of bits and parts—mostly lines and geometric shapes. You can edit an object by moving, resizing and reshaping its parts. An object hidden by another, like the square at left, still exists on its own "layer"; you can bring it to a front layer to see it whole again.

Frames (see p. 136) and QuickTime movies are also objects, which means that they answer to Drawing mode menus.

Painting mode pictures are just collections of screen dots, or "pixels." If you paint over a square in such a picture, it is lost forever because there is only one layer. As the computer needs a lot of memory to remember the color of all the pixels, you can't do serious color painting with less than 8 MB of RAM.

51

DRAW BASICS

Choosing *Drawing* in the *New Document* dialog box (see p. 8) creates a document with Draw tools and menus.

You can also start from within a Text or Spreadsheet mode document by clicking the *Show Tools* button. The menus change into the Draw menus and you may apply the various Draw features to your work of art as if you were inside the Draw mode.

ARROW

In Text or Spreadsheet mode, this tool lets you move Draw objects and Frames. In Database, it moves *Layout* objects (see p. 106).

In Draw mode, the Arrow tool is the default tool.

You revert to it each time you've finished working with another tool—unless you have double-clicked the other tool when selecting it.

You can select several objects at once by dragging the Arrow Pointer to draw a *Selection Rectangle* around them, by Command-dragging (in which case, objects do not have to be entirely within the rectangle), or by Shift-clicking.

A very useful feature: you can move objects one pixel at a time by pressing the arrow keys. When Autogrid is on (see p. 61), objects move one grid unit at a time.

CROSSBAR

This tool lets you create a Spreadsheet Frame inside a document belonging to another mode (see p. 130).

DRAWING TOOLS
See opposite page.

FILL/PEN PALETTES
See p. 54.

TEXT

When this tool is selected in Draw or Spreadsheet mode, the Pointer becomes an I-beam.

You can just click and type anywhere, or drag the I–beam pointer to define a text "frame" before typing. In any case, once written, the text becomes an "object" that you can move and resize.

PAINT

This tools lets you create a Paint mode Frame inside a document belonging to another mode.

EYEDROPPER

Clicking an object with this tool lets you "pick up" the fill and pen attributes of the object. This takes less time then choosing fill and pen settings on the palettes.

When you Command-click an object with the Eyedropper Pointer, the current fill and pen settings are applied to the object.

SELECT, MOVE, RESIZE

Objects have four or eight "handles" (see p. 58). When the arrow Pointer is inside an object, clicking selects it and dragging moves it. Dragging a corner handle changes the size or shape of the object.

52

You may feel a bit clumsy with these tools at first, but it does not really matter, as you can always edit Draw mode objects—by dragging their handles, choosing the **Reshape** command (see p. 59), changing their Fill and Pen attributes and applying the various Draw transformations to them (see p. 62).

The Paint mode is less forgiving!

STRAIGHT LINE

Drag from one point to another to draw a line. Shift-drag to constrain it to horizontal, vertical or an angle defined in Preferences (see p. 58).

ROUNDED RECTANGLE

You can define the radius of rounded corners. See p. 66.

ARC

Drag to draw one fourth of an oval inscribed inside the selection rectangle. The **Reshape** command (see p. 59) lets you change the angle of the arc.

This oval was filled automatically by the active Fill color. The other objects on this page seem not to be filled because their Fill is white (default color) or transparent.

FREEHAND

When you drag with this tool, the program creates a "smoothed" zigzag that follows your movement, more or less.

REGULAR POLYGON

This is a proper regular polygon. You define the length and angle of a side by dragging. You can choose the number of sides (default is six—see p. 66).

RECTANGLE

Drag to define the diagonal of the rectangle.
Shift-drag to draw a square.

OVAL

Dragging defines a selection rectangle. The oval is inscribed inside the rectangle.
Shift-drag to draw a circle.

POLYGON/ZIGZAG

With this tool you do not drag, but click here and there to define a series of linked straight lines. When you Option-click, the lines are not straight but "smoothed." You can stop drawing either by clicking the starting point, which creates a polygon, or by double-clicking anywhere.

Thus, this tool should not be called *Polygon* (a closed figure) but maybe *Zigzag*.

BEZIGON

With this very special tool you click and drag and click and drag to define *Bézier Curves* (from the name of a French engineer).

You reshape the curve by moving *Anchor Points* and *Control Handles* (see p. 59).

Option-click to draw straight lines. This is a basic tool of illustration programs like Adobe Illustrator.

DRAW BASICS

Objects that have an "inside," like rectangles, ovals and arcs, can be filled with a color/pattern. ClarisWorks also fills objects drawn with the Zigzag and Bezigon tools, often in a surprising way. Objects drawn with the Freehand tool are not filled.

Pen color and/or pattern apply to lines and to object outlines.

The seven Fill and Pen pop-up menus become floating "palettes" when dragged away.

FILL SAMPLE
"Preset" fill, which appears inside this box, is chosen when no object is selected and defines the look of new objects. Choosing a fill for a selected object does not change the preset fill.

PEN SAMPLE
Active Pen width, color and pattern appear inside this box.

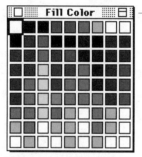

COLOR PALETTE
The standard palette shows 81 colors, with white as default for Fill and black as default for Pen. See also opposite page.

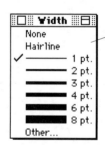

PEN WIDTH
Default is 1 pt. *None* means "no outline" (for plain rectangle, etc.) *Hairline* is 0.25 pt for LaserWriter.

PATTERNS
The first pattern is *Transparent*. The second one, *Opaque*, is selected by default.

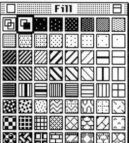

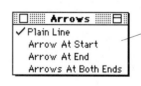

ARROWS
Only Straight Lines can become arrows.

GRADIENTS
While the black-to-white gradients on the first two lines may be useful in some cases, the color gradients are samples that you must adapt to your taste. See opposite page.

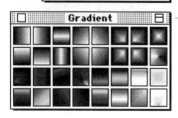

RED & BLUE
This is what the palette looks like on a Macintosh set to black and white.

You can't edit the 81-color palette; to create custom colors, you must replace it with the *Editable 256-Color Palette* (in Palette Preferences, see p. 23). This 16x16 palette is so big that there is no room to show it here!

To display the Color/Gradient/Pattern Editor, just double-click a color/gradient/pattern that you don't plan to use.

Color Wheel

To create a color, click anywhere on the wheel, or enter numbers into the boxes, or click the tiny arrow buttons near the boxes. The scroll bar at right controls brightness.

The upper part of the rectangle at top left shows the new color; the lower part shows the color you started with. Clicking the lower part reverts to the original color.

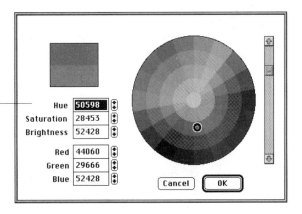

Patterns

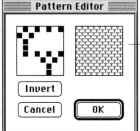

Click inside the box at left to show or hide pixels. The box at right shows the pattern. *Invert* means negative: black becomes white, white becomes black.

Gradient

Drag the tiny solid handle around the perimeter of the circle to define the angle of the gradient (you can also enter a number into the *Angle* box); drag the hollow handle along the radius to change the "focus position."

The Circular and Shape Burst sweeps have similar controls. You can play fascinating (though probably useless) games with these tiny handles. Try it!

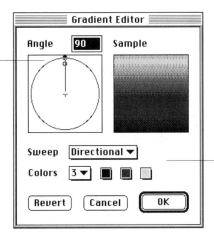

Sweep, Colors

The **Sweep** pop-up menu gives you a choice of **Directional**, **Circular** and **Shape Burst**.

The **Colors** menu lets you choose between two, three and four colors.

55

DRAW BASICS

This very simple picture showcases some of the tools and functions of the Draw mode.

While ClarisWorks lacks some features of dedicated graphics programs like ClarisDraw and Adobe Illustrator—e.g., you can't "write on a curve" or set the number of steps of a gradient—there is no real limit to what a serious artist could create with the Draw and Paint modes.

COLOR/PATTERN
This picture was made on a Macintosh LC with sixteen colors.
The face is filled with a brown color and a dotted pattern.

PASTE
The picture is selected and copied. The "Sakura" text document (see p. 9) is opened.
The Insertion Point is put after "genius" and the Return key is pressed to create a new paragraph. Then the **Paste** command is chosen in the **Edit** menu.
The picture is treated by the text module as a character.
Here, as it is alone on the line, it is also a paragraph, which can be formatted as a paragraph—e.g. centered, etc.

Every child is born a genius

Einstein International School
Hasegawa Bldg., 5-3 Maruyama-cho, Shibuya-ku, Tokyo 150 Japan, 03-3780-6641

SCALE
The picture was selected inside the Text document and reduced 50% with the **Scale Selection...** command of the **Options** menu.

56

The Einstein picture is a collection of objects. They are shown separated below for demonstration purpose, but they were drawn more conventionally: the oval object first, then the other objects over and around it.

OVAL
A run-of-the-mill oval for Einstein.

POLYGON/ZIGZAG
This shows the hair as it was created with the Zigzag tool. It was then "smoothed," duplicated and flipped horizontally.

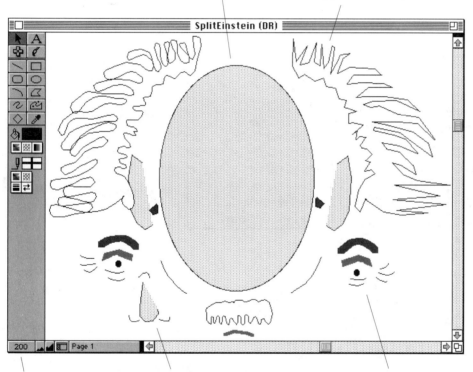

ZOOM
Scale has been set at 200 to draw the picture. The zoom tool is one of the great boons of computer drawing.

FILL
Since they were also made with the Zigzag tool, the ears and nose can be filled, even though they are not closed. Automatic closing of "polygons" can be requested in Preferences.

FREEHAND LINES
Eyebrows and eyes are just thick Freehand lines.

In Draw mode, the commands of the Edit menu apply to selected objects. The selection process is described on p. 52.

CUT/COPY/PASTE

When a Text object is selected with the Arrow tool, you cut/copy/paste the whole text object—and **Format** menu commands change the whole text. When the Text tool is on, you can select some characters as if you were in Text mode and cut/copy/paste them—also, change their attributes, or spell-check the selection.

DUPLICATE

A duplicated object appears in front of the original object, with a slight rightward and downward offset.

This is a basic Draw feature, and you should definitely remember the obvious keyboard shortcut. Moving a just duplicated object defines the offset for the next duplication. A very powerful feature—see p. 61.

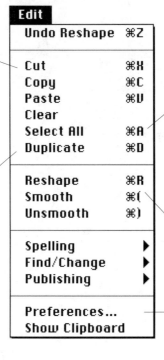

SELECT ALL

When no tool is active, this selects all objects.

A strange feature: when a tool is active, only objects created with that tool are selected. Note that the Freehand, Polygon and Bezigon tools are considered one tool for this feature: when one of them is active, all objects created with one of the three tools are selected.

RESHAPE/SMOOTH

See opposite page.

PREFERENCES

See dialog box below.

OBJECT SELECTION

By default, a selected object has four handles. Eight handles are useful for Frames: mid-side handles let you change one dimension of the selected object at a time.

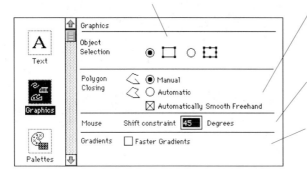

AUTOMATICALLY SMOOTH FREEHAND

The Freehand tool is similar to the Polygon/Zigzag tool, but it creates too many points. Whether *Automatic Smoothing* is on (default option) or off doesn't make much difference.

SHIFT CONSTRAINT

This angle applies to lines Shift-drawn with the Line, Polygon and Bezigon tools. Default is 45 degrees.

FASTER GRADIENTS

This is a display option: gradients don't look as good, but they display faster. It doesn't affect printing.

When you choose **Reshape** after selecting an object created with the Polygon/Zigzag, Arc, Freehand, Bezigon or Regular Polygon tool, *Anchor Points* appear and let you reshape the object much more precisely than by dragging its four (or eight) handles. For a regular polygon, the anchor points are its vertices; for a Zigzag or Bezigon, the points you clicked to create the object; for an arc, its extremities.

Unsmooth

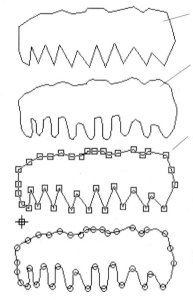

This is the original mustache, drawn with the Zigzag tool.

Smooth

Here, the **Smooth** command has been chosen.

Reshape

Square anchor points appear—or round anchor points if the line is smoothed—and the pointer takes a crosshair shape. Every single anchor point can be moved.

ClarisWorks anchor points are very big and tend to crowd each other. Going to 200% or 400% scale helps things somewhat.

You can add an anchor point by clicking the line with the crosshair Pointer, select an anchor point by clicking it (it becomes black), and remove a selected anchor point by pressing Backspace.

When you Option-drag an anchor point, it moves and grows Bezigon *Control Handles* (see p. 53) at the same time.

In fact, a Zigzag, a Freehand shape, a Regular Polygon and a Bezigon are all Bezigons. When you unsmooth a Bezigon, it loses its Control Handles and becomes a Zigzag. You can also Option-click a Control Handle to supress it.

You can connect two objects belonging to the Bezigon category: cut or copy object A, select object B, choose **Reshape** and **Paste**. Object A is connected to the beginning of object B (to the end if you press Option when you choose **Paste**). Try it!

A Strange Thing Happened to Einstein's Mustache

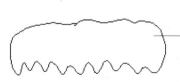

Einstein was initially drawn in ClarisWorks 1.0, then the document was converted to ClarisWorks 2.0.

This is the old smoothed mustache. Compare it to the second picture above.

The unsmoothed mustache was the same, but, since there were no Bezigons in version 1.0, smoothing did not use Bézier equations as in version 2.0 and the smoothed mustache is different.

Thus, if you convert a drawing from version 1.0 to version 2.0 (e.g. from Windows to Mac), you should expect to see changes!

59

DRAW MENUS

When a Text object is selected with the Arrow Pointer, choosing commands in one of the submenus below applies attributes to *all words* in the object.

Activating the Text tool and selecting characters inside the text with the I-beam Pointer calls the Text mode menus, including **Font**, **Size** and **Style**. You can then apply attributes selectively.

RULER
See opposite page.

FONT, ETC.
Font, **Size**, **Style** and **Text Color** submenus are similar to Text mode menus (see p. 38).
Alignment and **Spacing** replace Text mode ruler icons.

HEADER/FOOTER
These commands add a text Header/Footer—*not* a Text object—to the Draw document.
You can create an object Header/Footer with the *Master Page* feature (see p. 65).

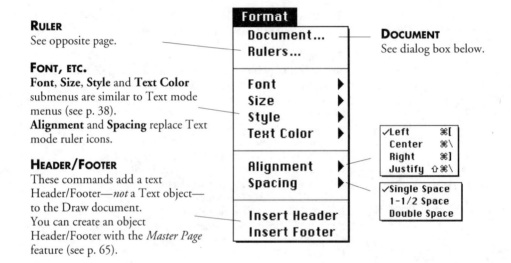

DOCUMENT
See dialog box below.

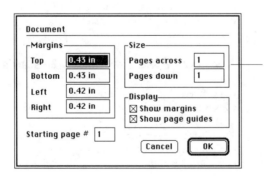

DOCUMENT
This dialog box is different from the *Document* dialog box in Text mode (see p. 36). Several pages can be created for a *Spread* or a slide show.

60

Rulers are very useful when you're creating charts or technical drawings. The marks on the ruler define dotted *Gridlines*.

In most cases (but not always—see below) the rulers' marks correspond to the *Divisions* of the invisible snap-to *Grid* which attracts objects when the **Align to Grid** command of the **Options** menu is on.

DIVISIONS

This number (between 1 and 512) applies to the invisible lines of the snap-to Grid. By default, there are 8 divisions per inch in Draw mode.

When it is possible, ruler marks reflect grid divisions—see below.

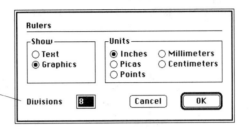

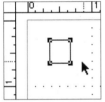

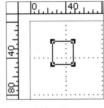

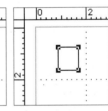

INCH/8 DIV.
Default ruler. Notice that the position of the arrow's tip appears as dotted marks on both rulers.

INCH/12 DIV.
Marks on rulers reflect invisible grid divisions.

POINT/8 DIV.
When you press an arrow key, the object moves by 1/8 or 0.125 pt. Ruler marks are located every 5 pt.

MILLIM./10 DIV.
When you press an arrow key, the object moves by 0.1 mm. Ruler marks every 2.5 mm.

CENTIM./10 DIV.
Here again, ruler marks reflect grid divisions.

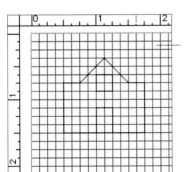

VISIBLE GRID

Until such a grid becomes a standard option, you have to make it yourself. Put it on a *Master Page* (see p. 64) and remove it before printing!

Creating the grid is easy if you remember a clever feature of the **Duplicate** command. Draw the first horizontal line; duplicate it; align line #2 precisely under line #1 by pressing the left arrow once; now, when you duplicate again, line #3 will be exactly under line #2, because the **Duplicate** command always repeats any custom offset you defined for the first duplication.

DRAW MENUS

While the **Edit** menu lets you change the shape of objects, the **Arrange** menu lets you change the position or other attributes of objects without modifying their shape.

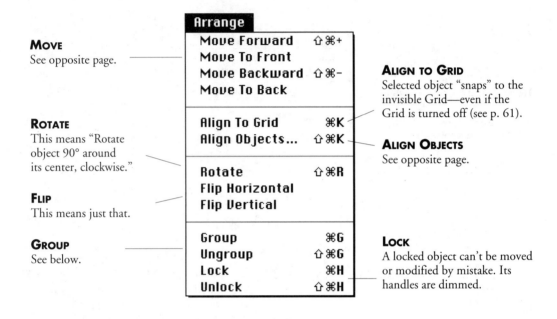

MOVE
See opposite page.

ROTATE
This means "Rotate object 90° around its center, clockwise."

FLIP
This means just that.

GROUP
See below.

ALIGN TO GRID
Selected object "snaps" to the invisible Grid—even if the Grid is turned off (see p. 61).

ALIGN OBJECTS
See opposite page.

LOCK
A locked object can't be moved or modified by mistake. Its handles are dimmed.

UNGROUPED
Four (or eight) handles per object end up hiding the whole picture.
Also, moving all the objects together is risky, as some pieces may decide to stay behind. Choosing the **Group** command is a good safety measure.

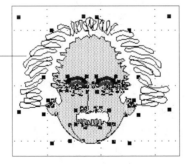

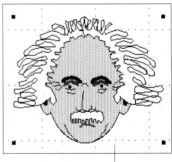

GROUPED
Several objects appear as one, with only four (or eight) handles.

62

Objects (including fields and layout text in Database mode documents) belong to tracing-paper-like layers.

Move Forward and **Move Backward** move an object one layer nearer or farther; **Move to Front** and **Move to Back** moves it to the nearest or farthest layer.

The little game with A, B and C below is quite easy, but may become harder with more objects.

You can align several selected object by choosing the **Align Objects...** command.

Default Draw shortcuts help you move and align objects.

THREE OBJECTS

Actually, each card is made of two grouped objects: a rectangle and a letter.

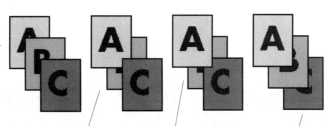

MOVE FORWARD

A is brought forward one layer. It moves in front of B, but stays behind C.

MOVE TO FRONT

Starting from the first picture at left, A is moved all the way to the front.

MOVE TO BACK

Starting from the second picture at left, C is moved behind B.

NONE

If you choose None in *Top to Bottom*, objects will not move vertically, but only horizontally.

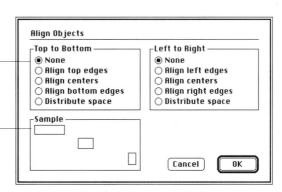

SAMPLE

The three rectangles in the *Sample* box move instantly to show what your choice of alignment looks like.

DRAW SHORTCUTS

Row 2, from left to right: Align top, left, bottom and right edges; Align centers horizontally and vertically; Move forward and backward; Irregular text wrap; Rotate 90°.

DRAW MENUS

The Options menu offers some typical computer art features, like an invisible snap-to grid and custom scaling. They won't turn you into Leonardo da Vinci, but they certainly make life easier at times.

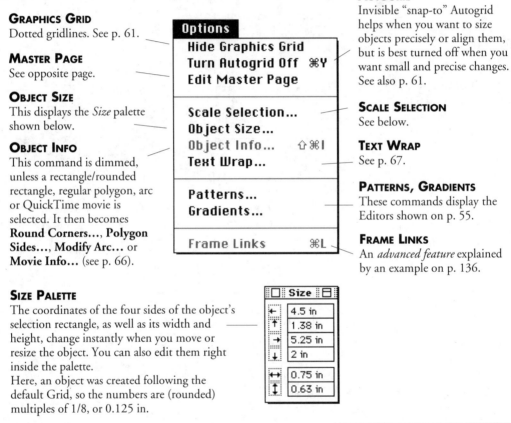

GRAPHICS GRID
Dotted gridlines. See p. 61.

MASTER PAGE
See opposite page.

OBJECT SIZE
This displays the *Size* palette shown below.

OBJECT INFO
This command is dimmed, unless a rectangle/rounded rectangle, regular polygon, arc or QuickTime movie is selected. It then becomes **Round Corners...**, **Polygon Sides...**, **Modify Arc...** or **Movie Info...** (see p. 66).

AUTOGRID
Invisible "snap-to" Autogrid helps when you want to size objects precisely or align them, but is best turned off when you want small and precise changes. See also p. 61.

SCALE SELECTION
See below.

TEXT WRAP
See p. 67.

PATTERNS, GRADIENTS
These commands display the Editors shown on p. 55.

FRAME LINKS
An *advanced feature* explained by an example on p. 136.

SIZE PALETTE
The coordinates of the four sides of the object's selection rectangle, as well as its width and height, change instantly when you move or resize the object. You can also edit them right inside the palette.
Here, an object was created following the default Grid, so the numbers are (rounded) multiples of 1/8, or 0.125 in.

SCALE
Dragging a handle lets you resize a selected object in a rough way. Note that you should Shift-drag for a horizontal, vertical or proportional resizing.
The **Scale Selection...** command lets you resize a selection more precisely. The selection can be a ClarisWorks object or collection of objects selected together, or an imported drawing.

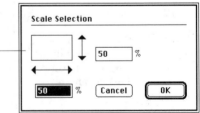

Master Page is a powerful Presentation and DTP feature.

A Draw page is in fact a transparent, tracing-paper-like sheet lying on top of a white background. Choosing the **Master Page** command hides the transparent sheet, so that you can draw (or write a Text object, e.g. *Confidential*, etc.) on the background.

There can be only one Master Page per document. It appears as a background behind all pages of the document.

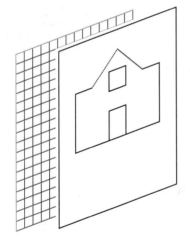

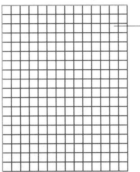

BACKGROUND

When you choose **Master Page**, you see only the background.

A Master Page may contain drawings, text objects, and Paint or Spreadsheet frames.

To delete items on the Master Page, select them and press Backspace.

FOREGROUND

After creating a background, you must choose **Master Page** again to see the foreground.

If **Page View** (in the **View** menu) is not active, you see only the foreground. This may be more convenient when you edit a text and do not need to see the background.

Though it is hidden, the Master Page appears in print.

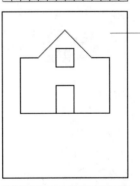

BOTH

When you choose **Page View**, the Master Page appears in the background. What you do on your foreground sheet does not affect it. For example, you might paste a scanned picture onto the Master Page, then trace it on your sheet, then delete the scanned model.

65

DRAW MENUS

The examples below show three versions of the **Object Info…** command, which correspond to the selection of a rounded rectangle, an arc and a QuickTime movie.

ROUNDED RECTANGLE

The first example shows a rectangle with *Round ends;* the second one shows a rounded rectangle with a 12 pt *Corner Radius.*

ARCS

When you draw an arc, its angle is always 90°. **Modify Arc…** lets you change the Start and Arc angles. The first example shows a simpler way to do it: choose **Reshape** and drag the ends of the arc.

The second arc has a Fill but unframed edges, the third one has frame edges but no Fill.

The rich *Pie Chart* was created with the Arc tool—with some duplicating and flipping and the help of the Zigzag tool.

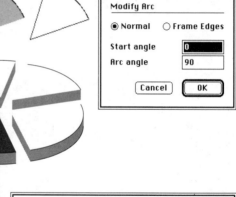

QUICKTIME MOVIE

QuickTime is a Macintosh movie format. You can open a QuickTime Movie as a separate Draw document, or insert it or paste it into an existing document.

The movie appears with a small *Control Badge* at bottom left. Click it to show the *Movie Control Bar* as on the example at right. When you click outside the picture, this Bar disappears. You can then select the movie as object, move it, resize it, and choose **Movie Info…**.

Note that what is imported is only the first picture of the movie *(Poster)* and the address *(Path)* of the movie file. The rocket won't blast off if the program doesn't find the movie file—e.g., if you've moved it to another folder.

Play/Stop   Step

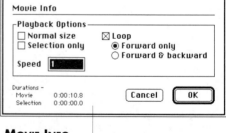

MOVIE INFO

Check *Normal size* to return a resized movie to its original size.

You can select part of the movie by Shift-dragging on the play bar.

Normal speed is 1. Enter a bigger number for a faster speed, a smaller number for a slower speed. When the speed is negative, the movie plays backwards.

Options: Info, Text Wrap

The *Text Wrap* feature lets you define the relationship between a text and an object. This works only with objects drawn, inserted or pasted onto a Text page. Not (alas) with a Text object in a Draw mode page.

As an object inserted or pasted at the Insertion Point into a text becomes a character, you should select the Draw mode's arrow tool before you insert or paste.

REGULAR

This is obviously the only possible way text can wrap around rectangular objects such as *Frames*.

A sad consequence: you can't create a nice *Irregular Text Wrap* around Paint pictures, since in Text mode they always come inside Frames.

The same caveat applies to a Text object on a Text page (e.g., a Drop Cap): only *Regular Text Wrap* is possible.

NO TEXT WRAP

In the default situation, there is no *Text Wrap* and the object appears in front of the text when inserted or pasted. The text just does not notice the object. Here, the object has been *sent to back* so that it does not hide the text.
Note that this Einstein has been redrawn in a paler shade!

IRREGULAR

Beautiful, isn't it? Note that such a Text Wrap looks good when the text alignment is *Justified*. You can also align the first column right and the second column left, as was done here.

67

Paint

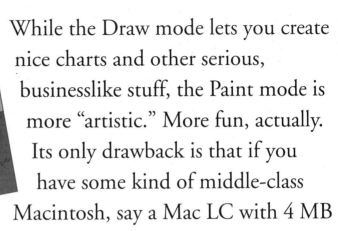

While the Draw mode lets you create nice charts and other serious, businesslike stuff, the Paint mode is more "artistic." More fun, actually. Its only drawback is that if you have some kind of middle-class Macintosh, say a Mac LC with 4 MB of RAM, you won't be able to paint much. As soon as you add nice colors to a picture or select it to apply some transformation, you get a "Not Enough Memory" message.

You should try to increase the memory allowed to the ClarisWorks application, by selecting the ClarisWorks icon, choosing **Get Info** in the Finder's **File** menu and replacing the default 950K by 2048K or so.

If this doesn't work, reduce the size of the document and choose a smaller number of colors in the *Monitors* Control Panel—16 is a good number.

For example, the picture above was made with four levels of gray only.

PAINT BASICS

When you enter Paint mode—by opening a Paint document, or by creating or clicking a Paint frame—you see all the tools of Draw mode, plus other tools specific to Paint mode.

Using a Draw tool in the Paint mode feels the same as in Draw mode, except that what you draw doesn't become an editable object but a collection of pixels. Thus you should define the color of a fill, the angles of an arc or the width of a line very carefully *before* you start drawing.

ARROW
This tool is useless inside a Paint document, but it lets you select a Paint *frame* as object.

SPREADSHEET
You can create a Spreadsheet frame inside a Paint document, but as soon as you click outside it or select another tool, it becomes a collection of pixels.

DRAW TOOLS
Lines, rectangles, etc. are pixels and have no handles. Zigzags can't be smoothed.
Double-clicking the Rounded rectangle, Arc or Regular polygon tools opens *Object Info* dialog boxes.

MAGIC WAND
Selects adjacent same-color pixels. See opposite page.

PENCIL
Default tool. Double-clicking lets you toggle between 100% and 800% scale. See p. 72.

SPRAY CAN
Double-clicking opens the dialog box shown on p. 73.

PALETTES
The 256-color editable palette is shown by default. The other palettes are the same as in Draw mode.

TEXT
When this tool is active, just click anywhere and write. You enter Text mode and can edit the text, but as soon as you click outside it or select another tool it becomes a collection of pixels.

PAINT TOOL
This tool is useless in a Paint document. It lets you create a Paint frame in other modes.

EYEDROPPER
Click to pick up color for Fill; Option-click for Pen color.

SELECTION
See opposite page.

BRUSH
Double-clicking opens the dialog box shown on p. 72.

PAINT BUCKET
See p. 73.

ERASER
Double-clicking erases the whole page. See p. 73.

PAINT TEXT IS FUN
Once text becomes Paint mode pixels, you can do all kinds of things to it. From left to right: superimpose letters of different colors, distort, fill with gradient.

You do not select a Paint mode picture by clicking it like a Draw object, but by surrounding it by a *Selection Rectangle* or *Lasso Loop*. You can also select a color slab with the *Magic Wand*.

You can move, cut, or copy a selection, and apply to it the commands of the **Transform** menu.

PIGGIES

The little pig was copied in a HyperCard demonstration stack and pasted into ClarisWorks. Many publishers sell collections of electronic pictures ("Clip Art") in various formats.

RECTANGLE, LASSO

The rectangle is easy to use because you just drag the pointer diagonally, but it selects a lot of useless white space.

The lasso selects only the picture, but you must drag the Pointer around the picture quite carefully. Note that the lasso loop closes automatically with a straight line when you release the mouse button. Command-dragging with the rectangle is another way to lasso a picture: it selects the picture only.

Double-clicking the Rectangle tool selects the whole page, double-clicking the Lasso tool or Command-clicking the Rectangle selects all the pictures.

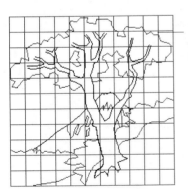

MAGIC WAND

Why would you select adjacent pixels of the same color? Not to flip or distort the selection. The most useful commands are probably **Lighten** and **Darken** (see p. 77).

Here's a trick.

A visible pale blue grid was created (or copied in Draw mode and pasted). By the way: in Paint mode, you duplicate a selection by Option-dragging it.

A Hiroshige picture was traced on lined paper, then drawn with the Zigzag tool, with the grid as a reference. Copying from one grid to another is a classical (i.e., pre-scanner) way of reproducing or enlarging pictures.

In the end, the grid was selected with the Magic Wand and deleted. As parts of it were not "adjacent" anymore, the Magic Wand was used several times.

HOT SPOT

The active part of the Magic Wand ("hot spot") is the center of the spark. Remember that if you select the wrong color, you can undo. To play it safe, enlarge the picture first.

PAINT BASICS

The best way to understand what these tools do is to experiment with them. Some people like the Pencil, while others prefer the Brush. You may find that the best way to create a good picture is to begin it in Draw mode, where you can do some preliminary editing, then copy it and paste it onto a Paint page. This is how the mouse on p. 2 was made.

Note that, while Draw tools retain their 45 degrees constraint in Paint mode, Shift-dragging Paint tools creates horizontal or vertical lines.

DOUBLE-CLICK
Double-clicking the Pencil Tool on the palette toggles the scale between 100 and 800%.

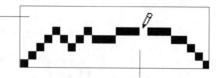

A PIXEL OR NOT A PIXEL
At 800%, the Pencil's special talent lets it add or remove pixels one at a time, as in this enlargment of Fuji San's top.

BLACK & WHITE
The pencil draws one-pixel-wide lines in the Pen color.
If its journey begins on the selected Pen color, it erases a line one pixel-wide.

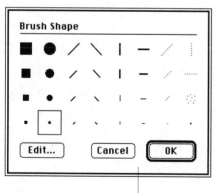

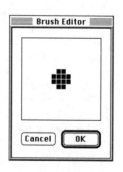

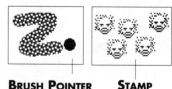

BRUSH POINTER
The Brush draws in the Fill color and pattern —although the Pointer stays black.

STAMP
Custom Einstein Brush is used as a one-click stamp.

BRUSH SHAPE
· Double-clicking the Brush tool displays the *Brush Shape* dialog box.
Clicking the *Edit...* button opens the *Brush Editor.*
Choose a Brush you don't use to change it into a custom brush!

72

Tools: Pencil, Brush, etc.

The Paint Bucket is a very satisfying tool, as long as you are very careful to use it inside a *closed* surface. Otherwise the paint spills all over the place and you must undo IMMEDIATELY. You must then enlarge to 400% or 800% scale and close the gaps in the surface's border.

The Spray Can is also very satisfying—but only on a big enough surface. This means that you may have to buy more memory before you can enjoy its power.

BUCKET

The bucket lets you fill an enclosed area or a solid shape with the active color and pattern or gradient.
Note that the bucket's "hot spot" is the tip of the paint flow.

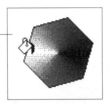

SPRAY CAN

The default shape of the Pointer can be seen at right. This sprays a cloud of dots in the active color. A double-click on the Spray Can tool opens the Spray Can Editor. *Dot size* means *Size of the Spray area* (between 1 and 72 pixels —default: 25). *Flow rate* is between 1 and 100 (default: 20). Clicking or dragging the arrow Pointer in the center area lets you test your choice.

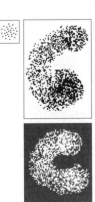
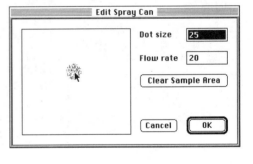

ERASER

At 100% scale, the Eraser Pointer is big and erases a wide surface. At 400% or 800%, the size of the Pointer is the same so it becomes more precise.
Erasing a surface is often done by selecting and deleting it.
A double-click on the Eraser tool clears the whole page.

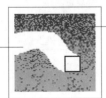

SPRAYED

The square picture that is being erased was created with the Spray Can. It became square when the Eraser shaved its sides. To erase along a straight line, press the Shift key.

73

PAINT MENUS

Remember: you can change the attributes of text only as long as you haven't clicked outside the text or selected another tool. It is safer to set the attributes before you start typing.

Once text becomes a Paint picture, you can color it with the bucket or the **Fill** command—more colors are available than for real text, actually, and also patterns and gradients. You can select it, move it, and transform it. See examples on p. 70.

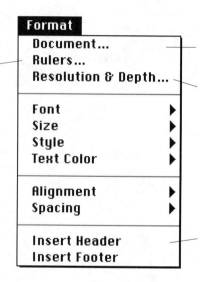

RULERS
This command displays the same dialog box as for Draw documents (see p. 61), but the default number of divisions is 9 instead of 8.

DOCUMENT
See below.

RESOLUTION & DEPTH
See opposite page.

HEADER/FOOTER
You can add a Header or Footer to the page and use it as a text editor, as its contents do not become pictures when you click elsewhere.
Edited text can then be copied and pasted onto the Paint page to become a picture.

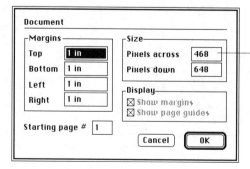

SIZE
Default document size is 468 x 648 pixels, or 6.5 x 9 inches at 72 dpi resolution, plus a one-inch margin all around. Maximum size is 2000 x 2000 pixels. When you open a Paint document in a low-memory situation (e.g., if another document is already open), the program may reduce its size.

Printing Paint pictures exactly as they appear on screen produces jagged edges—because screen pixels are BIG. The standard screen resolution is 72 dpi (dots per inch), so the size of a pixel is 1/72 inch. The feature below lets you draw in such a way that the picture can be printed at the LaserWriter's resolution of 300 dpi, with tiny 1/300 inch dots and no jaggies.

Note that you get the same result by printing a picture at a 24% scale (by entering this number into the *Reduce or Enlarge* box of the printing dialog box, see p. 28): 1/72 inch screen pixels become 1/300 inch LaserWriter dots.

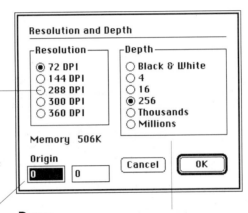

RESOLUTION

When you choose 288 dpi, elementary picture dots become four times smaller than screen pixels (288 = 72x4). This means that pictures become four times smaller, and actually the whole page becomes smaller. Try it! As the tiny dots are smaller than screen pixels, you can't see them on screen. You must increase scale to 400% to work with regular screen pixels.

ORIGIN

The *Origin* option appears in the dialog box for Paint frames only. It lets you define the position of the picture inside the frame: you enter the coordinates of the part of the picture you want moved to the frame's top left corner.

DEPTH

Description of a black & white picture requires one *Bit* per pixel (with a value of 0 or 1); 4 colors require 2 bits; 16 colors 4 bits, etc. The memory needed—displayed at left—is doubled every time. According to the ClarisWorks manual, a full-size high-depth picture needs 13 MB of memory. You need a big Mac and a printer with extra memory.

LOW- AND HIGH-RES RABBITS

A 288 dpi rabbit, a 72 dpi rabbit. This sweetie was scanned from a Hokusai "Manga" (comics), then imported via the **Insert...** command of the **File** menu.

PAINT MENUS

The commands of this menu apply to a selection, so they become available only when you select an area with the Selection Rectangle, the Lasso or the Magic Wand.

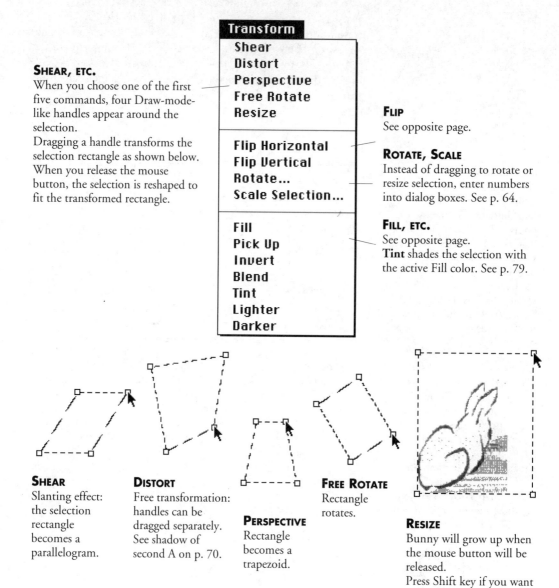

SHEAR, ETC.
When you choose one of the first five commands, four Draw-mode-like handles appear around the selection.
Dragging a handle transforms the selection rectangle as shown below. When you release the mouse button, the selection is reshaped to fit the transformed rectangle.

Transform
Shear
Distort
Perspective
Free Rotate
Resize

Flip Horizontal
Flip Vertical
Rotate...
Scale Selection...

Fill
Pick Up
Invert
Blend
Tint
Lighter
Darker

FLIP
See opposite page.

ROTATE, SCALE
Instead of dragging to rotate or resize selection, enter numbers into dialog boxes. See p. 64.

FILL, ETC.
See opposite page.
Tint shades the selection with the active Fill color. See p. 79.

SHEAR
Slanting effect: the selection rectangle becomes a parallelogram.

DISTORT
Free transformation: handles can be dragged separately. See shadow of second A on p. 70.

PERSPECTIVE
Rectangle becomes a trapezoid.

FREE ROTATE
Rectangle rotates.

RESIZE
Bunny will grow up when the mouse button will be released.
Press Shift key if you want proportional resizing.

Perhaps you should skip this gray page and discover the transformations on your screen in glorious color by trial and error!

FLIP

Horizontal (left) and vertical (right).
Note that you can flip by choosing the **Resize** command and dragging the handles "backward."

FILL

The left rabbit is filled with the Paint Bucket. The right one is selected with the lasso and filled with the **Fill** command.
For solid selections (e.g. Magic Wand selections) the result is the same.

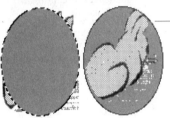

PICK UP

An oval is selected with the lasso and carried over the rabbit (left). While it is still selected, the **Pick Up** command is chosen.
The oval picks up what is under it. As it is still selected, it can be moved away. In this example, the oval has been duplicated first, so the picked-up rabbit could be installed inside its Easter egg.

INVERT, BLEND

Inversion changes black into white, light gray into dark gray, and any color into its complementary.
The **Blend** command decreases the contrast between two adjacent colors by creating a thin band of intermediate color. The picture becomes slightly fuzzy. Can't see much happening to the gray rabbit at right, though.

LIGHTER, DARKER

The rabbit has tiny gaps in its ears (that were closed only for the bucket fill example). Thus, when you select it with the lasso, the inside of the rabbit is not selected and the **Darker** command only darkens its outline and shadow.
These two important commands can be accessed by buttons on the default Paint shortcuts palette (see next page).

PAINT MENUS

The Paint mode's *Autogrid* is even more invisible than the Draw mode's, since it is not marked by dotted lines. See a custom visible grid on p. 71.

The Shortcuts palette is really useful in Paint mode. The default palette is shown below. More shortcuts: *Turn Autogrid On/Off, Pickup,* etc. are available. See p. 147.

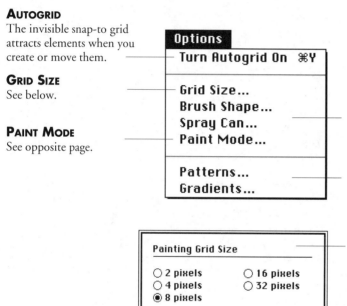

AUTOGRID
The invisible snap-to grid attracts elements when you create or move them.

GRID SIZE
See below.

PAINT MODE
See opposite page.

BRUSH SHAPE, SPRAY CAN
These commands display the dialog boxes that can be seen on pp. 72 & 73. The usual way to display them is to double-click the Brush or Spray Can tool.

PATTERNS, GRADIENTS
Pattern and Gradient Editors, shown on p. 55, can be opened by double-clicking a Pattern or Gradient on its palette.

PIXELS
By default, the Painting grid has nine divisions per inch. As one inch equals 72 pt or screen pixels (at least, on most monitors), a division is 72/9 = 8 pixels. This is reflected by the default ruler marks. Notice the dotted marks showing the pencil's position.

SHORTCUTS PALETTE
Paint shortcuts on row two, from left to right: Rotate 90°, Opaque mode, Transparent pattern mode, Tint mode, Lighten, Darken, Tint command, Fill command, Blend, Invert.

If you want to play with these options, you should display the Shortcuts palette and use its buttons. It would be very tedious to open the dialog box below every time you wanted to switch from one *Painting Mode* to another.

TRANSPARENT PATTERN

Opaque is the default mode: a picture filled with a pattern covers anything it is drawn upon.

When the *Transparent pattern* option is checked, the white pixels in a pattern are transparent. This applies to the fill of a rectangle, oval, zigzag, bezigon, regular polygon and to the trace of the brush *when you are drawing*—not retroactively.

Using a brush with a Transparent pattern is very effective for relief and shading. See the mouse on p. 2.

TRANSPARENT RABBIT

The white rabbit has been selected with the Lasso and moved over the gray one. It is transparent because it has gaps in its ears.

Thus, you can make a figure transparent by opening a gap in its outline. A thin white straight line, for example, does the trick; you can close it at 400% or 800% scale later.

TINT

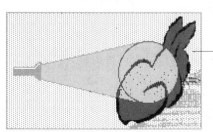

This picture is very impressive in full color!

When the yellow circle is drawn, it "tints" the rabbit underneath. Yellow is the active Fill color.

Two tangents to the circle are then drawn. The lower one defines a small triangular area near the rabbit's rump. Selecting this small triangle with the Magic Wand and choosing the **Tint** command tints it also with the active yellow color. Completing the picture is easy.

A strange side-effect: in Tint mode, when you Option-drag a selection to duplicate it, the picture that stays behind is tinted.

79

Spreadsheet

It is said that the Macintosh moved from the home of writers and journalists to the offices of Fortune 500 companies when Excel, a powerful spreadsheet program, appeared.

The Spreadsheet mode of ClarisWorks offers you some of that power. Actually, if you need to perform basic calculations, like adding rows and columns of numbers, ClarisWorks is not less effective than a dedicated spreadsheet program.

Even if you don't want to juggle numbers, you should leaf through the following pages if you ever need to insert tables in a Text or Draw document, as ClarisWorks tables are *Frames* (see p. 136), which belong to the Spreadsheet mode.

SPREADSHEET BASICS

A new ClarisWorks spreadsheet has 40 columns and 500 rows. Of course, most of the time, you won't need that many.

The box defined by the intersection of a column and a row is a cell. The "active" or "current" cell is marked by a heavy border.

CANCEL
This button is called "Cancel Entry."
It empties the Entry Bar, but not the cell; the Delete key empties both.

ENTER
This button is called "Accept Entry."
When you click it, press the Enter key, or activate another cell, the data is verified (or calculated if the Entry Bar contains a formula) then entered into the active cell.

TITLE
"SS" means Spreadsheet mode.

ENTRY BAR
Text, numbers or "formulas" can be entered here.
The word "January" will appear in cell B2 when the Enter key is pressed.

CELL ADDRESS
The address—column and row—of the active cell.

COLUMN HEADERS
The **Display...** command of the **Options** menu lets you hide these letters —before printing, for example. See p. 97.

ROW
Default height is 14 pt, but can be changed (see opposite page).

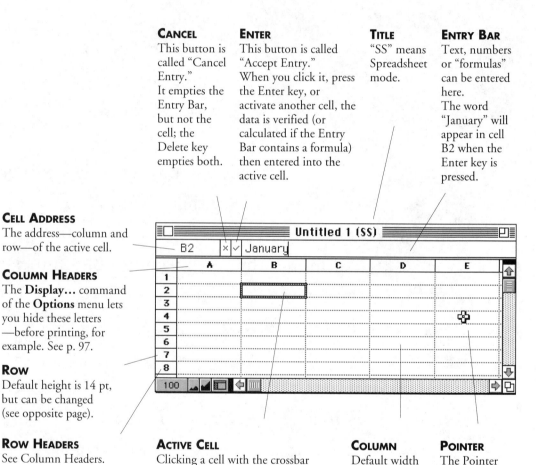

ROW HEADERS
See Column Headers.

ACTIVE CELL
Clicking a cell with the crossbar Pointer makes it active.
You can activate a neighboring cell by pressing the arrow keys or the following keys:
Tab (right), Shift-Tab (left), Return (down), Shift-Return (up).

COLUMN
Default width is 72 pt, but can be changed (see opposite page).

POINTER
The Pointer takes this crossbar shape over the cells.
It becomes an I-beam over the Entry bar.

82

This page introduces elementary Spreadsheet gymnastics. Resizing and selecting exercises can be practiced on empty cells, as below, or on cells that contain data.

You resize whole columns or rows—for aesthetic purposes or to adjust for the length/style/size of the data entered into the cells.

Selecting cells, columns or rows is necessary if you want to change the format of the data, to cut/copy it, etc.

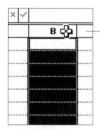

RESIZE POINTER

The pointer takes this double-arrow shape between two row or column headers.

Dragging right or left in the example below will resize column A. **Row Height** and **Column Width** can also be set with **Format** menu commands.

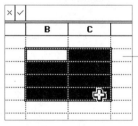

SELECTED COLUMN

Clicking on a column or row header selects the whole column or row. This does not activate any cell beyond the first one.

When several adjacent rows or columns are selected together by dragging over their headers or by shift-clicking, they can all be given the same size: just set any one of them to the chosen size.

SELECTED RANGE

Dragging along a diagonal selects a rectangular range of cells. Selecting a range of cells is a good idea when you want to enter data into these cells: pressing the Enter key then activates cells in the range from left to right, row after row; pressing the Return key activates them from top to bottom, column after column.

SELECT ALL

Clicking the intersection of the row and columns header bars selects the whole spreadsheet. When the Option key is held down, the spreadsheet is selected only as far as the farthest filled cell.

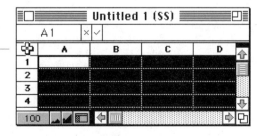

SPREADSHEET BASICS

Although the ClarisWorks spreadsheet mode can do many things, it is likely to be used most often to add rows and columns of numbers. Even powerful, dedicated spreadsheet programs such as Excel are often used only for this humble task.

This page shows you how to do it, with a double-barreled, step-by-step approach.

ADD ONE BY ONE

Click the cell where you want the sum to appear, then write the = sign, which signals the program that a *formula* will be built.

After that, clicking a cell makes it part of a sum, which is the default formula.

This method is okay if you want to add a few numbers, but it is not very convenient if you need to add one hundred numbers.

1
Click cell C1 and type the = sign.

2
Click cell A1.

3
Click cell B1.

4
When you click the Enter button or press the Enter key, the result appears inside cell C1.

PASTE A FUNCTION

Click the cell where you want the sum to appear, then write the = sign, which signals the program that a formula will be built.

Then, choose the **Paste Function...** command in the **Edit** menu and select the SUM function.

Drag over a range of cells or write their references (i.e., the two "anchor points" of the range separated by two periods, A1..W35) to define the arguments of the function.

1
Type =, then paste function SUM or write SUM().

2
You can enter the argument of the function by clicking each cell, as in the other method…

3
… or you can drag to enter a range of cells, or write A1..B1.

4
Happily, the end result is the same: 2+3=5.

Formulas

If you have mastered the addition on the opposite page, here is something more challenging.

Cell F5 contains the formula = B5+C5+D5+E5. This formula is repeated in cells F6, F7, F8, and F9 (with the **Fill Down** command of the **Calculate** menu, see p. 93), but the program adjusts it automatically: it becomes = B6+C6+D6+E6 for cell F6, etc.

If you change the contents of cell B5, all the formulas which refer to this cell address will be affected, so that the contents of cells F5, B10 , F10, B16 and F16 will change instantly.

SUBTRACT

When you click cells, plus (+) signs appear in the Entry bar, as a default sum is built.
If you want minus (-) signs, you have to press the minus key.

TITLE

The title was entered into cell A1 (maximum length is 255 characters), and a large Gill Bold font was chosen.
The title spills over into empty neighboring cells.

ALIGNMENT

This cell is centered; numbers are usually aligned on the right.
Format commands work in the traditional way.

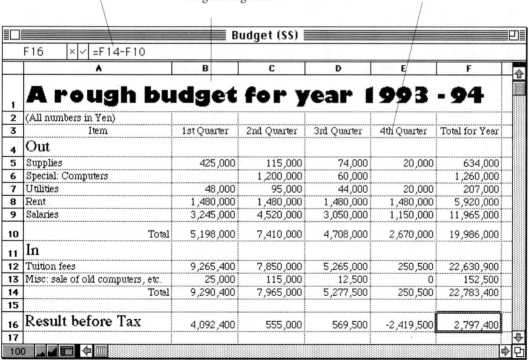

	A	B	C	D	E	F
	F16	×✓ =F14-F10				
	A rough budget for year 1993 - 94					
2	(All numbers in Yen)					
3	Item	1st Quarter	2nd Quarter	3rd Quarter	4th Quarter	Total for Year
4	Out					
5	Supplies	425,000	115,000	74,000	20,000	634,000
6	Special: Computers		1,200,000	60,000		1,260,000
7	Utilities	48,000	95,000	44,000	20,000	207,000
8	Rent	1,480,000	1,480,000	1,480,000	1,480,000	5,920,000
9	Salaries	3,245,000	4,520,000	3,050,000	1,150,000	11,965,000
10	Total	5,198,000	7,410,000	4,708,000	2,670,000	19,986,000
11	In					
12	Tuition fees	9,265,400	7,850,000	5,265,000	250,500	22,630,900
13	Misc: sale of old computers , etc.	25,000	115,000	12,500	0	152,500
14	Total	9,290,400	7,965,000	5,277,500	250,500	22,783,400
15						
16	Result before Tax	4,092,400	555,000	569,500	-2,419,500	2,797,400
17						

Budget (SS)

100

SPREADSHEET BASICS

Selecting a range of cells with some words and numbers, then choosing the **Make Chart...** command in the **Options** menu, displays the *Chart Options* dialog box below.

Once you've chosen a chart type (default is Bar chart) and clicked OK, the chart appears over the spreadsheet.

TITLE
The contents of the top-left cell become the default Title.

LEGENDS
The contents of the first column become the default Legends.

SELECTED RANGE
The spreadsheet on p. 85 has been changed slightly for this example.

1993-1994	4th—93	1st—94	2nd—94	3rd—94
Supplies	473,000	1,410,000	178,000	40,000
Rent	1,480,000	1,480,000	1,480,000	1,480,000
Salaries	3,245,000	4,520,000	3,050,000	1,150,000

ROWS AND COLUMNS
As there are fewer rows than columns, the program casts rows as *Series*. This means the chart will show three series of bars four times.

AXIS
This button lets you add a label for the axis; put tick marks inside, outside or across the axis; remove the grid lines; set a Minimum value for the axis (e.g., if the values are between 1 and 1.1 million, minimum could be 900,000 instead of 0).

CHART OPTIONS
This dialog box changes when you click one of the *Modify* buttons. You can edit an existing chart from this dialog box—choose **Modifiy Chart...** in Draw mode's **Options** menu or double-click the chart. You can also use Draw tools and commands, as a chart is a Draw object. Note that it is a grouped object and that you should ungroup it first.

SERIES
You can show one series of data as bars and another one as a line; display the value for each bar ("Data label").

LABELS
Change, delete or move Title; delete or move Legends.

GENERAL
Change the Spreadsheet range; choose columns for series instead of rows; force the program to consider the first column or row as labels/legends even when it contains numbers (e.g., 1992, 1993, 1994).

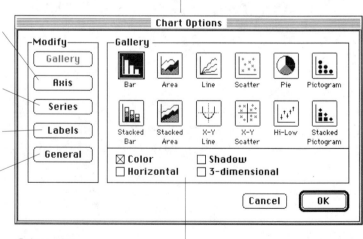

COLOR, ETC.
These options change when you select another chart type in the *Gallery*. A note to Claris: this dialog box sorely lacks an *Apply* button.

Charts

The charts below are graphic representations of the data on the opposite page.

As long as the chart stays inside the spreadsheet, it is "linked" to the original cell range. When you change numbers or formats in the cell range, the chart reflects the changes instantly. A chart pasted as object into another document loses its link with the cell range.

CHART

The Title, Legends and horizontal-axis text of this default chart have the same character formats as the data in the cells. The format for the vertical-axis values is provided by the program: Geneva 9.
You can resize the chart by dragging its handles with the arrow pointer.

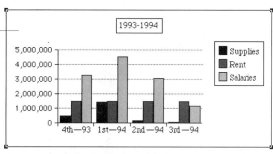

IMPROVED BUT STILL A CHART

The *Chart Options* dialog box was displayed by double-clicking the Title.
Title and Legends were moved; then the bars were improved with a *Shadow* and a *3-D Effect*.
A silly-looking *Axis Label* was added to the vertical axis.
The whole frame was selected as object and tinted with a gradient Fill. The Title and the Supplies legend were then selected and changed in the same way.

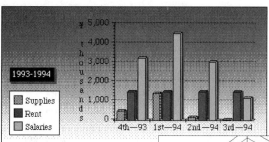

REAL 3-D

This is what Excel calls a 3-D chart—very different from the cosmetic 3-D option of ClarisWorks.

NOT A CHART

Title and Legends were removed; then the chart was copied and pasted into a Draw document. There it was ungrouped so that its various items could be edited. Notice that Legends are now Text objects that can be rotated and moved anywhere.
Vertical lines were added to the bars for a light/shadow effect.

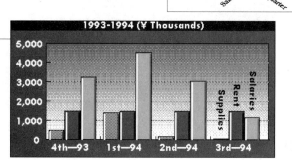

SPREADSHEET BASICS

Double-clicking a chart's border displays the *Chart Options* dialog box (see p. 86), where you can choose another chart type in the *Gallery*. When you click OK, the chart is changed instantly. This is true as long as the chart stays where it was created—in a spreadsheet document or in a frame.

An example of a chart inside a Frame is given on p. 132.

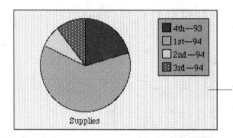

PIE CHART

This classical Pie Chart corresponds to four columns but only one row of data. The *Series* option of the *Chart Options* dialog box lets you put unreadable *Data Labels* on the slices. Creating small Text objects is much better.

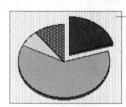

EXPLODED SLICE

You "explode" (or "restore") a slice by Option-clicking its legend. This pie is also "tilted" and has a shadow.

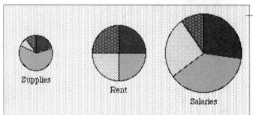

MULTIPLE PIES

These *Multiple pies* correspond to the four columns and three rows of data on p. 86. By default, multiple pies are the same size. Here, they have been "scaled" to reflect the total cost per quarter.

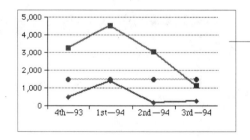

LINE CHART

This chart is a cousin of a bar chart, but it can't be made "3-D." You can change or remove the *Data Point* symbols. A *Scatter Chart* is similar to a Line chart, with Data Point symbols but no lines.

Some other chart types are not shown here: Bars can be *stacked;* an Area chart is similar to a Line chart, but areas can be stacked, like bars; a Hi-Low chart is a peculiar kind of chart often used to track stock prices. Try them all!

X-Y LINE CHART

This is the kind of chart used in college mathematics or physics, with one line, numbers on both axes—and two rows of numbers in the original range.

An X-Y Scatter Chart has Data Point symbols but no line.

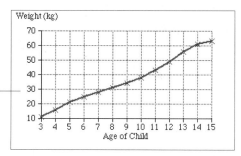

PICTOGRAM CHART

Pictograms, like the houses at right, are superimposed over bars.

Selecting a Legend lets you apply a Fill (here, a gradient) to the bars. You can suppress the bars by filling them with a Transparent pattern.

Here, unreadable Data Labels were replaced by Text objects.

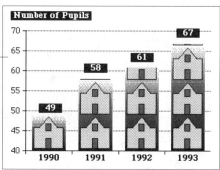

PICTOGRAMS: HOW TO DO IT

Draw a picture and copy it. (Avoid Paint images in low memory situations.)

Choose *Pictogram* (or *Stacked Pictogram*) in the Gallery of the Chart Options dialog box.

Click the *Series* button to display the options at right.

The Sample box shows the default pictogram, an arrow. Select this box and choose the **Paste** command in the **Edit** menu.

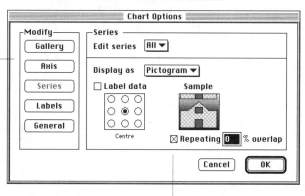

REPEATING

The example above shows a "repeating" pictogram. Non-repeating pictograms are stretched to fit the length of the bars—this works fine with an arrow, for example.

SPREADSHEET MENUS

In the Spreadsheet mode, the **Cut/Copy/Paste** commands act upon the *contents* of a cell or range of cells; the cells themselves do not move. You can also copy and paste the *format* of a cell.

If you want to move cells *and* contents, you should first create new cells by choosing **Insert Cells...** in the **Calculate** menu (see p. 95), then paste the contents into the new cells.

CUT/COPY/PASTE

Let's say range A2..B5 is selected. If you choose **Copy**, then activate cell R20, then choose **Paste**, the contents of cells A2..B5 will appear inside cells R20..S23, replacing the former contents of this range.

Activating one target cell is enough: you don't have to select a range before pasting.

When cell contents are formulas, pasting modifies them, because the program adjusts formulas to their location (see p. 85 —formulas are "relative"). =A1+A2 may become =F8+F9, for example. The value changes accordingly.

PASTE SPECIAL

See dialog box below.

When a cell contains a formula, you can choose to paste the cell's value without bringing over the formula.

Before you can *transpose* a selected range of cells, i.e. exchange rows and columns, you must cut or copy the range.

CLEAR

This command deletes the contents of a cell or range *and* its formats.

The Backspace key deletes only the contents.

PASTE FUNCTION

This opens the dialog box below, where you can choose a Spreadsheet functions like SUM, AVERAGE, etc. (see p. 84). A full list of ClarisWorks Spreadsheet and Database functions is given on p. 142.

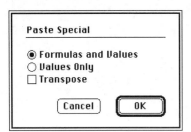

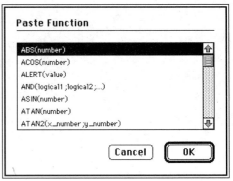

The **Format** menu lets you change Font, Size, etc. of selected cells, and adjust the column width and row height precisely.

The **Borders...** command lets you print some of the lines around the cells. This helps you create clear, easily readable tables—e.g., spreadsheet frames inside Text or Draw documents.

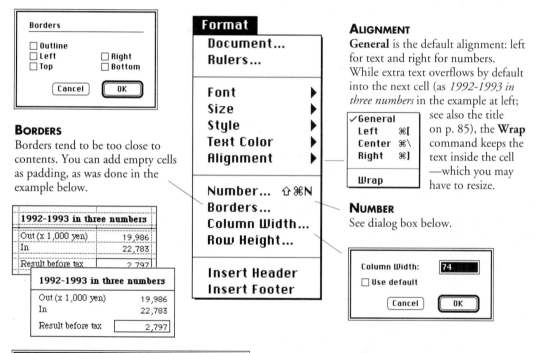

BORDERS

Borders tend to be too close to contents. You can add empty cells as padding, as was done in the example below.

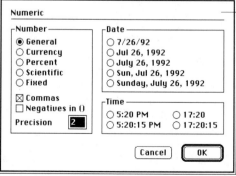

ALIGNMENT

General is the default alignment: left for text and right for numbers. While extra text overflows by default into the next cell (as *1992-1993 in three numbers* in the example at left; see also the title on p. 85), the **Wrap** command keeps the text inside the cell —which you may have to resize.

NUMBER

See dialog box below.

NUMBER AND DATE FORMATS

The *General* (default) format adapts the number of decimal places to the width of the cell. Maximum is 16 decimal places. This maximum precision is used for computation, whatever the display shows. Useless zeros are dropped: 5.00 is shown as 5. *Currency* (meaning $), *Percent* and *Fixed* numbers are displayed by default with a two-decimal place precision—e.g., 5 is shown as 5.00. You can choose any number of decimal places between 0 and 15. Uncheck *Commas* to display 1994 as 1994 and not 1,994.

SPREADSHEET MENUS

In dedicated spreadsheet programs, commands like **Move...**, **Fill Right/Down** and **Insert/Delete Cells...** belong to the **Edit** menu. In ClarisWorks, the **Edit** menu tries not to change too much from one mode to another, so the above commands are regrouped arbitrarily with calculation commands in the **Calculate** menu.

FILL RIGHT/DOWN
See opposite page.

SORT
See p. 94 and palette below.

INSERT/DELETE CELLS
See p. 95 and palette below.

CALCULATE NOW, AUTO
Changing the value of a cell changes the value of all the cells linked by formulas to the original cell.
In the p. 85 example, changing cell B5 changes cells F5, B10, F10, B16 and F16.
Here, this takes less than a second, but in a bigger spreadsheet with many formulas it could take quite a while.
Turning off **Auto Calc** lets you enter or change values in several cells much faster.
You then update the whole spreadsheet whenever you want, in one shot, by choosing **Calculate Now**.

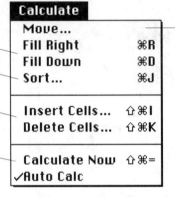

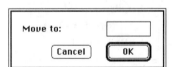

MOVE
Selecting a range of cells and "moving" it with this command (see dialog box below) is basically the same thing as cutting and pasting. However, if the range contains formulas, cutting and pasting changes the formulas, while moving doesn't.
There is a very convenient shortcut for moving: just Option-Command-click a cell to "move" the selected range to that cell.
You can't "move" a range from one document to another; you must cut and paste.

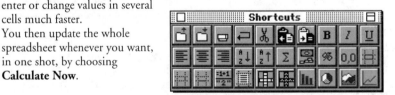

SPREADSHEET SHORTCUTS
Row 2: Align left, center & right. Sort ascending & descending. Calculate Sum of selected rows or columns. Set format to currency, percent & commas. Show outline border.
Row 3: Show right & bottom border. Show or hide formulas. Wrap text. Insert & delete row or column. Create bar, pie, area & line chart.

While "moving" cells can be compared to cutting and pasting, "filling" is similar to *copying* and pasting.

Filling is a much more important function than moving, however, as it can be used to copy formulas. See the first example below. The second example shows that you can fill several columns at the same time.

If the range is not empty, the data it contains is replaced by the replicated values.

	A	B	C	D	E	F	
3	Item	1st Quarter	2nd Quarter	3rd Quarter	4th Quarter	Total for Year	
4	Out						
5	Supplies	425,000	115,000	74,000	20,000	=B5+C5+D5+E5	=B5+C5+D5+E5
6	Special: Computers		1,200,000	60,000			=B6+C6+D6+E6
7	Utilities	48,000	95,000	44,000	20,000		=B7+C7+D7+E7
8	Rent	1,480,000	1,480,000	1,480,000	1,480,000		=B8+C8+D8+E8
9	Salaries	3,245,000	4,520,000	3,050,000	1,150,000		=B9+C9+D9+E9
10	Total	=SUM(B5..B9)					=B10+C10+D10+E10

=SUM(B5..B9)	=SUM(C5..C9)	=SUM(D5..D9)	=SUM(E5..E9)

FILL RIGHT

Here, the formula is entered into cell B10. Cells B10 to E10 are selected, and the command **Fill Right** is chosen. The formula is replicated in each of the three selected cells to the right.

FILL DOWN

The formula is entered into cell F5. Cells F5 to F10 are selected. When the command **Fill Down** is chosen, the formula fills the selected range.

It is very important to understand that this formula means "add the values of the four cells to the left," so that the formula reads =B5+C5, etc. on row 5 and =B6+C6, etc. on row 6.

18	Menus				
19	Monday	Soup	Rice		Fruit
20	Tuesday				
21	Wednesday				
22	Thursday				
23	Friday				

18	Menus				
19	Monday	Soup	Rice		Fruit
20	Tuesday	Soup	Rice		Fruit
21	Wednesday	Soup	Rice		Fruit
22	Thursday	Soup	Rice		Fruit
23	Friday	Soup	Rice		Fruit

SOUP & RICE

In this example, there are no formulas, but "constant" data: "Soup," "Rice," and "Fruit." The **Fill Down** command is used simply to copy the data downward through the selected range. The empty column is to be filled by hand every day with the *Plat du Jour.*

SPREADSHEET MENUS

By default, the **Sort...** command first sorts words in alphabetical order, then numbers in ascending order.

If you want to "unsort" a range of cells, here is a precaution you should take before sorting: add an extra column to the range, fill it with numbers in ascending order, and sort it with the range. To unsort, just choose the first cell of this column as the order key and sort.

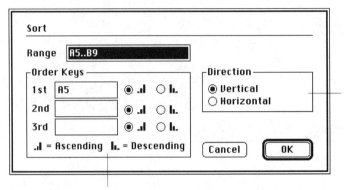

DIRECTION

With A5 as key, the selected range is sorted along column A if the *Vertical* button is checked.

You can choose to sort it along row 5 by checking the *Horizontal* button.

KEYS

Let's say you're sorting a range which contains last names in column A and first names in column B.

If the first order key is A5, the last names will be ordered alphabetically.

Choosing B5 as second key means that *Smith, Marilyn* and *Smith, Ronald* will be sorted according to their first names.

See a similar process for the fields of a database on p. 118.

DEFAULT SORT

If you select this range of cells, choose the **Sort...** command and click OK in the dialog box, the sort "key" will be the active cell, A5. The cells of the A column will be ordered alphabetically: Rent, Salaries, Special: Computers, etc.

5	Supplies	425,000
6	Special: Computers	0
7	Utilities	48,000
8	Rent	1,480,000
9	Salaries	3,245,000

CUSTOM SORT

If what you actually want is to order the cells of the B column from the biggest number to the smallest, as here, you should replace A5 with B5 in the Order Keys box and check the *Descending* button.

5	Salaries	3,245,000
6	Rent	1,480,000
7	Supplies	425,000
8	Utilities	48,000
9	Special: Computers	0

Calculate: Sort, Insert

Inserting cells is different from moving or pasting cells: existing cells are not replaced by the new ones, but pushed to the right or downward. Similarly, deleting cells moves existing cells left or up. The example below shows five cells being inserted.

Normally, this command is used to insert entire columns or rows. Note a clever shortcut: if you select some columns or rows before choosing the **Insert Cells...** command, as many new columns or rows as were selected appear and push the selected ones right or down. The dialog box *is not displayed*.

Deleting columns or rows is similar.

Insert Cells

○ Shift Cells Down
○ Shift Cells Right

[Cancel] [OK]

Delete Cells

● Shift cells up
○ Shift cells left

[Cancel] [OK]

DELETE
If some cells refer to deleted cells, their formulas are replaced by the error message "#Ref!"

INSERT
Oops! The empty cells between Rice and Fruit, for the *Plat du Jour,* have been forgotten.

Cells D20..24 are selected and the **Insert Cells...** command is chosen. The default option, *Shift Cells Down*, would push "Fruit" to cells D25..29.

Shift Cells Right is checked and the OK button is clicked: "Fruit" is sent to cells E20..24.

"Fruit" would also be displaced to E20..24 if the entire D column were selected and a new column inserted. Cells D1..19 would then also be displaced to E—the whole spreadsheet would be changed.

A new column is always 72 pt wide.

	A	B	C	D	E
19	Menus				
20	Monday	Soup	Rice	Fruit	
21	Tuesday	Soup	Rice	Fruit	
22	Wednesday	Soup	Rice	Fruit	
23	Thursday	Soup	Rice	Fruit	
24	Friday	Soup	Rice	Fruit	

	A	B	C	D	E
19	Menus				
20	Monday	Soup	Rice		Fruit
21	Tuesday	Soup	Rice		Fruit
22	Wednesday	Soup	Rice		Fruit
23	Thursday	Soup	Rice		Fruit
24	Friday	Soup	Rice		Fruit

95

Default font is Geneva 9. This prints as Helvetica on most LaserWriters, so the printed page won't look exactly like the screen display.

You might as well choose a LaserWriter-compatible font, like Helvetica or Times, as your default font. To view it on-screen without a magnifying glass, you'll want to change the size, or increase the view scale slightly. Times 12 is a good choice: it reads well on screen, and fits nicely in the default cell.

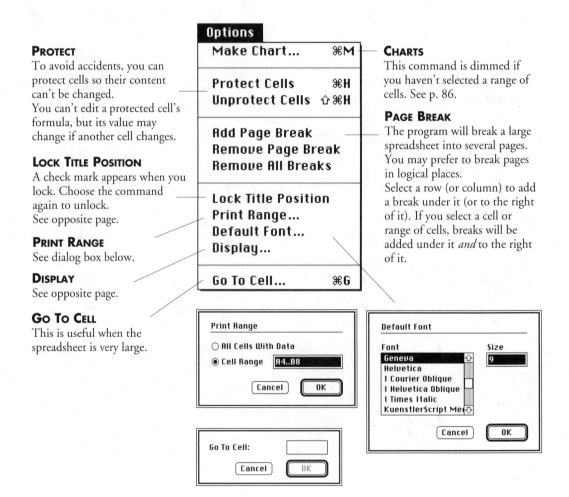

PROTECT
To avoid accidents, you can protect cells so their content can't be changed.
You can't edit a protected cell's formula, but its value may change if another cell changes.

LOCK TITLE POSITION
A check mark appears when you lock. Choose the command again to unlock.
See opposite page.

PRINT RANGE
See dialog box below.

DISPLAY
See opposite page.

GO TO CELL
This is useful when the spreadsheet is very large.

CHARTS
This command is dimmed if you haven't selected a range of cells. See p. 86.

PAGE BREAK
The program will break a large spreadsheet into several pages. You may prefer to break pages in logical places.
Select a row (or column) to add a break under it (or to the right of it). If you select a cell or range of cells, breaks will be added under it *and* to the right of it.

Options

Make Chart...	⌘M
Protect Cells	⌘H
Unprotect Cells	⇧⌘H
Add Page Break	
Remove Page Break	
Remove All Breaks	
Lock Title Position	
Print Range...	
Default Font...	
Display...	
Go To Cell...	⌘G

Print Range
○ All Cells With Data
● Cell Range A4..B8
[Cancel] [OK]

Go To Cell: [   ]
[Cancel] [OK]

Default Font

Font / Size
Geneva   9
Helvetica
I Courier Oblique
I Helvetica Oblique
I Times Italic
KuenstlerScript Me...
[Cancel] [OK]

Options

The first picture below compares two features: **Lock Title Position** and "splitting.".

The *Display* dialog box lets you show or hide Grid lines, column and row headers. These useful elements help you see cell addresses at a glance, resize rows and columns, etc. You may want to hide some of them before printing, however, or to replace dotted grid lines with solid lines—especially if you are printing not a full spreadsheet, but a "frame" inside a Text or Draw mode document (see p. 130).

Display options apply to the whole spreadsheet—not to a selected range of cells.

SPLIT VIEW, LOCKED TITLES

The window was split vertically and the right pane was scrolled. Then Row 3 was selected and the **Lock Title Position** command was chosen. The vertical Scroll bar only scrolls from row 4 on, as if the window were split between rows 3 and 4. There is a difference between locking titles and splitting the window: rows 1 to 3 are locked—you can't edit them.

GRID LINES

See the *Borders* example on p. 91 for visible and hidden grid lines.

FORMULAS

See formulas displayed on p. 93. If the spreadsheet seems to make mistakes when calculating, it means that *you* have made a mistake. Displaying the formulas helps you find it.

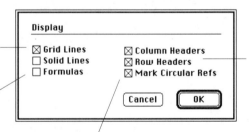

HEADERS

Headers refers to the row of letters above the spreadsheet and the column of numbers to the left of it. The **Format** menu also lets you add a text Header; these buttons do not apply to it.

CIRCULAR REFERENCE

A *Circular Reference* is a classical mistake. Cell B5 says =A3+B3, and cell B3 says =B5*10. Thus, when calculating, the program is trapped in a loop. Circular references may not be so easy to see when there are many complex formulas. ClarisWorks marks them (unless you uncheck the button) by surrounding the data with dots and displaying an alert box.

97

Database

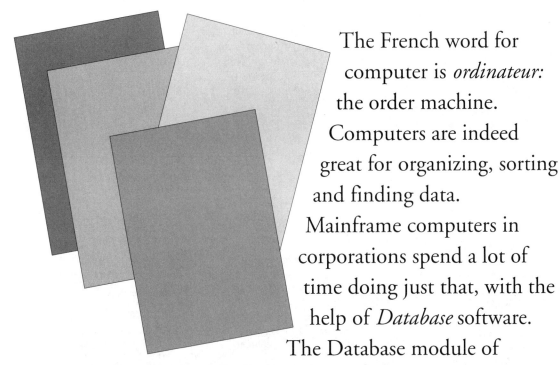

The French word for computer is *ordinateur:* the order machine. Computers are indeed great for organizing, sorting and finding data. Mainframe computers in corporations spend a lot of time doing just that, with the help of *Database* software. The Database module of ClarisWorks is a simplified, yet powerful, version of another Claris program, FileMaker Pro. It is quite separate from the other modules, and you can't link it to other modes with *Frames.*

A special kind of link does exist between Text and Database documents in the process of *Mail Merge,* explained on p. 134.

DATABASE BASICS

A *Database* is a place where you keep information that you want to organize or sort according to certain criteria.

An address book is a classic example. You probably own a paper address book, organized according to last names; with an electronic address book, you could not only retrieve all the names beginning with the letter G, but also all the addresses in a certain city, etc.

DEFINE FIELDS

As you'll recall, creating a new ClarisWorks document begins with the *New Document* dialog box (see p. 8).

When you choose *Database*, this large dialog box is displayed, as you need to define *Fields* for the various items you want to enter into the database.

See more about fields and *Options* on p. 116.

This dialog box can be displayed at any time—to modify, delete or create fields—by choosing the **Define Fields...** command in the **Layout** menu.

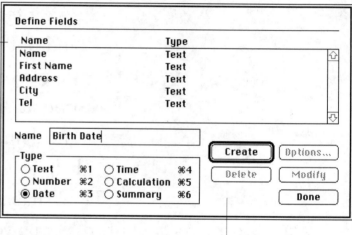

FIELD NAME

Write a name here and choose a field *Type*.

When you click *Create*, the name and type are entered into the big box above.

When you have created all your fields, click *Done*.

DEFAULT

When the *Done* button in the Define Fields dialog box is clicked, the program displays this default *Record* showing all the fields and their names.

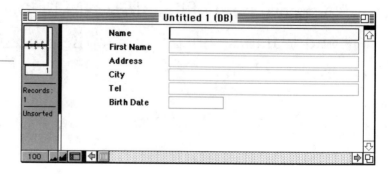

Here is what our database looks like after some working over.
The fields and their names were moved and resized in *Layout*
mode (see p. 106).

A Database *Header* was added with the **Define Part...**
command of the **Layout** menu. A regular text Header (where
time, date, and page # can be entered) may also be created with
the **Insert Header** command of the **Format** menu.

Three more records were created (**New Record**, **Edit** menu),
and data was entered into the three first records.

BOOK
Clicking the upper or lower part of the *Book*
activates the previous or next record.
The number of the active record is shown at
bottom right. See p. 102.

DB
"DB" means
Database.

RECORD
This is the first of
four *Records*.

ACTIVE RECORD
A black bar on the
left marks the active
record.
You can select an
entire record by
clicking outside a
field. You can cut or
copy a selected
record. To delete it,
you do not press the
Backspace key, but
choose the **Clear**
command.

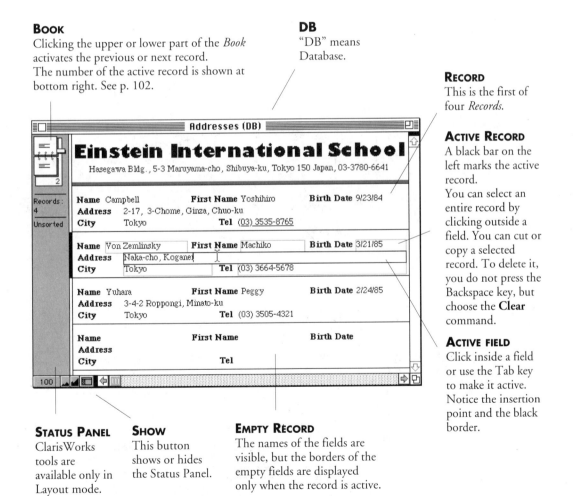

ACTIVE FIELD
Click inside a field
or use the Tab key
to make it active.
Notice the insertion
point and the black
border.

STATUS PANEL
ClarisWorks
tools are
available only in
Layout mode.

SHOW
This button
shows or hides
the Status Panel.

EMPTY RECORD
The names of the fields are
visible, but the borders of the
empty fields are displayed
only when the record is active.

DATABASE BASICS

The Database mode of ClarisWorks itself has three modes: Browse, Find, and Layout.

You see a default database as soon as you have defined fields, but you must go to *Layout* mode if you want to improve its look. This is often done by some database wizard, so that most users are familiar with only the *Browse* and *Find* modes.

Browse mode lets you create records and enter data into them, move from one record to another (see below), and create, modify, and delete fields.

BEGINNING
Out of 4 records, the active one is #1.
The upper page of the book is empty.
Clicking the lower page displays record #2.
The bookmark is at the top.

END
The active record is #4.
The lower page of the book is empty. Clicking the upper page displays record #3. The bookmark hits bottom.

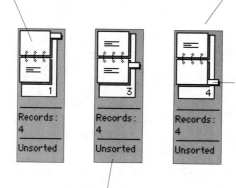

BOOKMARK
Dragging this cursor lets you browse through records.
This is fast, but not very precise in a large database.

MIDDLE
The active record is #3. Clicking the upper page of the book displays record #2; clicking the lower page displays #4.
The bookmark is a little more than half-way down.
Pressing Command-Return or Shift-Command-Return also activates the next or previous record; as a bonus, the Insertion Point moves to the *same field* in the new active record.

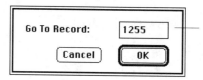

GO TO
In a large database, choosing the **Go To Record...** command in the **Organize** menu lets you reach a record quickly, provided you know its number.

Entering data into fields is usually a straightforward process, but it has some quirks (see below).

Although you can activate a field by clicking it, moving from one field to the next is most easily done with the Tab key. The *Tab Order* feature lets you define which field is actually the "next" one when you press Tab (see p. 115). Pressing Shift-Tab activates the previous field.

CONTENTS AND DISPLAY

You can enter as many as 500 characters into a text field.

You see them all when the field is active (see first example below), but when it is inactive, the display is limited to the borders defined in the layout (second example).

You must resize the field in Layout mode if you want to see and print the whole text (here, the two addresses).

FORMAT

The default text format for a field—font, size, style, etc.— is defined in Layout mode, but you can change the format of selected text in Browse mode.

Here, text is underlined to warn users that there is more in the field than meets the eye.

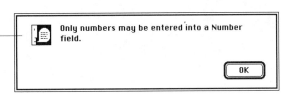

NUMBER FIELD

Use a Number field if you intend to refer to its data in a "calculation" field (see p. 110).

A Number field is limited to one line and 255 characters.

If you want to mix text and numbers but avoid this Alert box, use a Text field instead of a Number field; the numbers are then read as text.

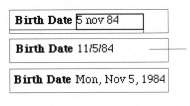

DATE FIELD

You get an Alert box similar to the one above if you try to enter a forbidden date like "xyz" or 11/32/84 into a date field, but "nov" is accepted for "Nov."

A date entered as 5 nov 84 is changed into the default format, 11/5/84, when you press the Tab or Enter key. You can change the default format in the **Options** menu of the Layout mode.

Children love the *Mon, Nov 5, 1984* format, which tells them which day of the week they were born on.

DATABASE BASICS

There are two different **Find** commands in Database mode.

With the **Edit** menu's **Find/Change** command (see p. 33), you can search a word such as "Shibuya" through all fields of all records, and replace it with another one if you want.

The **Layout** menu's **Find** command, specific to Database mode, displays all records in which the Address field contains the word "Shibuya" and hides the other records.

REQUEST

Choosing the **Find** command in the **Layout** menu displays a blank record called a *Request*.

When "Shibuya" ("shib" would be enough) is entered into the Address field and the *All* button is clicked, all the records where the field contains "Shibuya" are displayed.

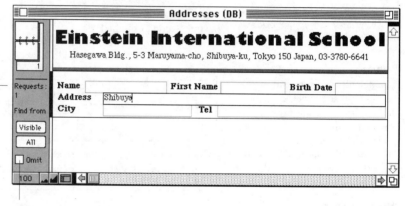

OMIT

When this button is checked, the Shibuya records are hidden rather than displayed.

FOUND

Two students live in the Shibuya ward. When their records are "found," you have a reduced database which acts as if it had only two records in total.

Choosing the **Show All Records** command in the **Organize** menu displays the full six-record database again.

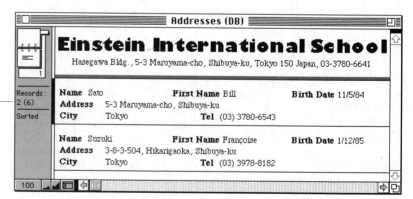

104

Once the Shibuya records have been found, you can look for younger children in this neighborhood by creating a date field request and clicking *Visible* instead of *All.*

It is faster, however, to combine these two steps into one with what is called an "And" search.

An "Or" search lets you find, for example, children who live in Shibuya *or* Harajuku.

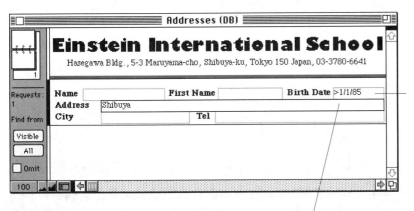

OPERATORS

The operators >, <, ≥, ≤ and = can be used with text, numbers, dates, and time. For example, you can find all names after letter G. This makes sense in the Name field, but wouldn't be possible in the address field above (see related discussion on sorting, p. 118).

AND

This "And" search uses One request, but several search fields. Pupils who live in Shibuya *and* were born after 1/1/85 will be found.
For an "And" search with only one search field (for example, >1/1/85 and <12/31/86), you should do two successive searches, with the second one restricted to the *Visible* records.

OR

An "Or" search uses several requests. You create a second request by choosing the **New Request** command—which replaces **New Record** in the **Edit** menu (see p. 150).
The second search field doesn't have to be the same as in the first request; there could also be several search fields in each request.

105

DATABASE BASICS

In Layout mode, all the Draw tools *and menus* are available. In this respect, the Database mode of ClarisWorks is more advanced than a dedicated database program like FileMaker Pro.

Fields are special Database mode objects. You can use the Draw tools and commands to move, resize, align and group fields—but you can't rotate or flip them.

The Header in the example below, as well as the field labels, are text objects.

PARTS

Body and Header are Layout *Parts*. A default layout only has a body. The **Insert Part...** command in the **Layout** menu lets you add other parts (see p. 112).

PART LABEL

Part labels (i.e., the gray rectangles marked *Header* and *Body*), as well as the horizontal lines which separate the parts, can be dragged up and down to resize the parts. Here, the *Body* part label hides the *City* field label. Selecting the hidden object and choosing the **Bring to Front** command in the **Arrange** menu would make it visible. The Part Label disappears in Browse mode and doesn't print.

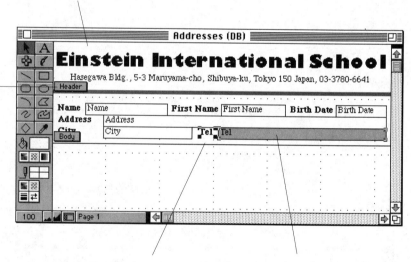

FIELD LABEL

A field label is a regular Draw mode Text object.

The **Format** menu lets you change its attributes: font, size, alignment, etc.

FIELD

As this field is selected, its handles are visible.

This field has been filled with a color. You can replace its default border ("None") with a visible one.

Finding and sorting data are two powerful features of the Database mode. Another feature, less obvious but also very powerful, lets you create several different layouts for the same database. Their names appear at the bottom of the **Layout** menu, so that you can display the data in different ways by switching between layouts.

NEW LAYOUT

This dialog box is displayed when you choose the **New Layout...** command in the **Layout** menu. *Standard* creates a default layout with all the fields (see p. 100); *Blank* creates a layout with no fields, where you add fields with the **Insert Field...** command (see p. 114); *Duplicate* creates a clone of the layout, which you can modify.
See below and p. 108 for *Columnar report* and *Labels*.

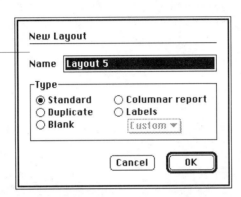

FIELD ORDER

This dialog box appears when you click the *Columnar report* or *Labels* button. You can choose which fields to include in the layout by selecting names in the Field List and clicking *Move*. See on p. 108 a Columnar report layout with Name, First Name, Address, and City fields (in this order); on p. 109, see Labels with Name, Address, and City fields.

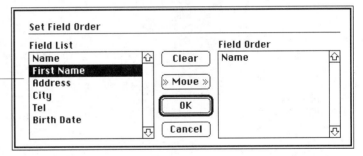

LABELS

When you choose the Labels option, a pop-up menu offers a list of standard Avery labels. You can design your own labels by choosing **Custom** in the pop-up menu and entering numbers into this dialog box.
Notice that the numbers measure a label *plus* the space between two labels.

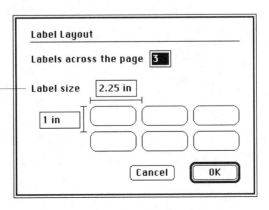

DATABASE BASICS

A columnar report layout is more compact than a standard layout, since the field labels are not displayed in every record, but only once in the Header.

You can delete or edit field labels in Layout mode, but not in Browse mode.

The field's name appears inside the field in Layout mode. It is replaced by data in Browse mode. The field name is not the same thing as the field label. You change it by choosing the **Define Fields...** command.

HEADER
While a standard layout only has a body, a columnar report layout always has a Header as well, where the field labels appear.

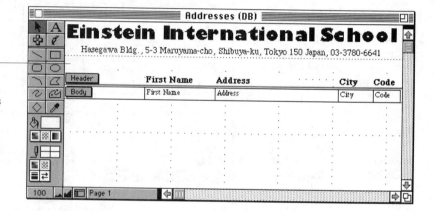

BROWSE MODE
Compare this Browse mode display of the above layout to the standard version on pp. 106-107: one report per line, and no birth date or phone number.

SORTED
A City Code field was added and used as First Key to sort the database, with Name as Second Key. See p. 118.

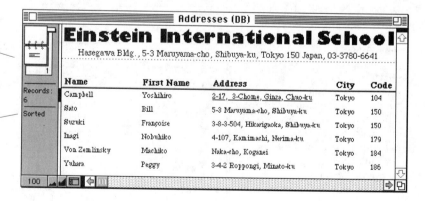

Layout: Columnar, Labels

A *Labels* layout shows only one label, but in Browse mode—and in *Page View*—labels cover the whole page and get printed accordingly.

ClarisWorks automatically compacts or "slides" fields in labels to give them a tighter, more professional look. See this clever trick—which doesn't appear on screen, but only on the printed page—demonstrated on p. 115.

LAYOUT MODE
You design the label only once, but this design will be repeated for all the labels.

BODY
You can drag the *Body* part marker and the horizontal separation line, but not the vertical limit between two labels. The only way to move it is to change the number of columns in the *Layout Info* dialog box.

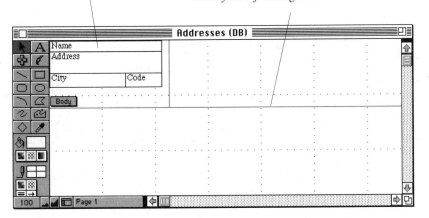

BROWSE MODE
Notice that this is the same *Addresses* database as on p. 101 and on the opposite page. You change the way the addresses are displayed by choosing a different Layout at the bottom of the **Layout** menu.

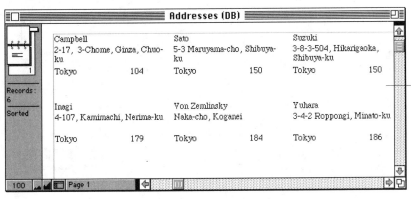

109

DATABASE BASICS

These two pages show the creation of a simple Calculation field called *Total*, where the sum of the values of three Number fields is displayed automatically.

Calculation fields use operators and functions to do things with the values of other fields. Adding Number fields is an obvious example, but you can also do "calculations" with Date fields and Date functions, or with Text fields and Text functions.

See the complete list of ClarisWorks functions on p. 142.

DEFINE FIELDS

A Text field *(Fees in)* and three Number fields *(1st Q, 2nd Q* and *3rd Q)* were created.
When you check the *Calculation* button, write the name *Total*, and click *Create*, the name doesn't appear right away inside the box as it does for Text/Number/ Date and Time fields. Instead, the dialog box below is displayed first, as a Calculation field can't exist without a formula.

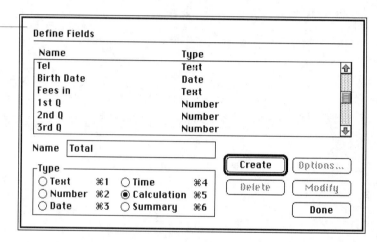

FORMULA

You can build a formula by clicking field names, operators, and functions inside their boxes.
You can also type it on the keyboard.
A field named City appears as 'City'.

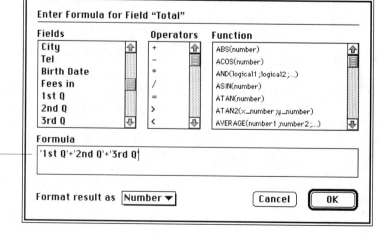

Calculation

The example below is a cousin of the Spreadsheet example on pp. 84–85, with fields instead of cells. The Spreadsheet and Database modes share most ClarisWorks Functions.

An example more specific to database programs is shown on the following two pages.

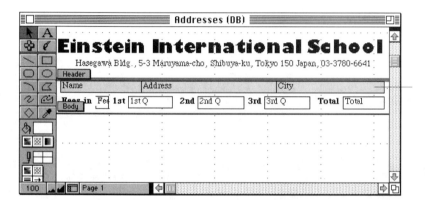

LAYOUT MODE
The labels of the new *1st Q, 2nd Q,* and *3rd Q* fields were shortened to *1st, 2nd,* and *3rd.* The labels of the Name, Address, and City fields were deleted to save space.

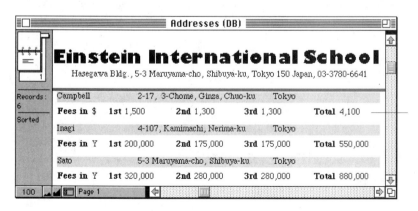

BROWSE MODE
As fees are sometimes paid from abroad in dollars, the Text field *Fees in* says $ or ¥.
Numbers are entered into the 1st, 2nd and 3rd fields. The program displays their sum in the *Total* calculation field.

111

DATABASE BASICS

While Calculation fields let you add (or average, etc.) several fields inside a record, Summary fields add (or average) the contents of one field throughout several records.

A Summary field can't belong to the body of a record, but must reside in a special part called a Sub-Summary or Summary part. So you must create both a field and a part.

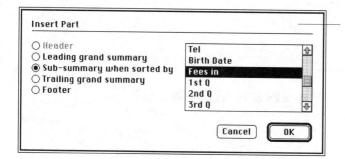

INSERT PART

A Grand Summary part adds values throughout the entire database. It can be located before the records to be summarized ("Leading") or after them ("Trailing").

A Sub-Summary part implies that the database is sorted into several subsets.

See opposite page.

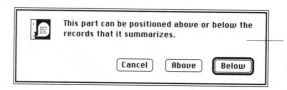

ABOVE/BELOW

The program does not give you a choice of Leading or Trailing sub-summary parts, but this dialog box is displayed when you check the *Sub-summary* button and click OK in the Insert Part dialog box.

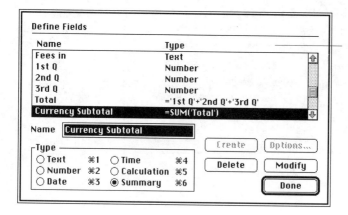

SUMMARY FIELD

Creating a Summary field is similar to creating a Calculation field: you must write a formula inside the Calculation dialog box. Here, the formula is SUM ('Total').

The result of the calculation depends on whether you locate the Summary field in a sub-summary or summary part.

See on the opposite page how the *Total* field is sub-summarized and the *Children* field is summarized.

In this slightly artificial example, the *Fees in* field, which contains either the symbol $ or ¥, is chosen as a sort key. When the database is sorted, records in dollars come first, and the sum of their totals appears in the *Currency Subtotal* summary field inside the sub-summary part. The records in yen are also sub-summarized.

A new field has been created, where the number of children of each family is entered. A summary field inside a trailing grand summary part shows the total number of children for the database (which has only six records here).

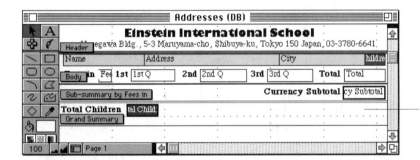

LAYOUT MODE

A sub-summary part and field appear only once in Layout mode. The fields are brought into the parts with the **Insert Field...** command.

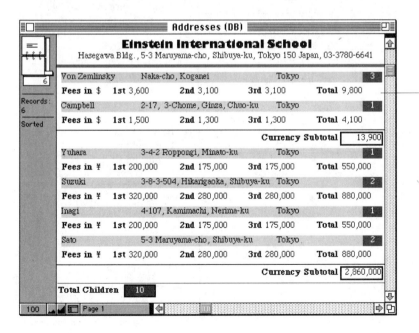

BROWSE MODE

This is what the Database looks like after:

1) It has been sorted with the *Fees in* field as key.

2) The **Page View** command is chosen. The sub-summary part and field appear at the bottom of each subset. The grand summary part and field appear only once, at the very end.

By the way, the formula of the *Total Children* summary field is SUM('Children').

113

DATABASE MENUS

The **Edit** menu is not shown here (see p. 150), but it does have some specific Database commands: **New Record** (replaced by **New Request** and **New Layout** in Find and Layout mode), **Copy Summaries** (the only way to transfer Summary data to another document, since you can't select data inside a Summary field), and **Duplicate Record**.

Most commands of the **Layout** menu are available even when Layout mode is not on. Some commands are available only in Layout mode: **List View**, **Insert Field...** and **Insert Part...**

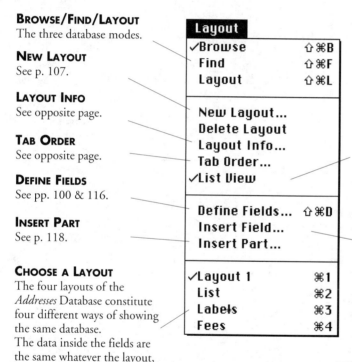

BROWSE/FIND/LAYOUT
The three database modes.

NEW LAYOUT
See p. 107.

LAYOUT INFO
See opposite page.

TAB ORDER
See opposite page.

DEFINE FIELDS
See pp. 100 & 116.

INSERT PART
See p. 118.

CHOOSE A LAYOUT
The four layouts of the *Addresses* Database constitute four different ways of showing the same database.
The data inside the fields are the same whatever the layout, but fields can be visible in one layout and hidden in another.

LIST VIEW
All the database examples in this book show records in List View, the default option. When the command is not checked, the program displays only one record at a time. You can't scroll from one record to the next, but you must use the book. One-record-per-screen view is a logical choice for one-page records like invoices, etc.

INSERT FIELD
When a layout doesn't include all the existing fields, this command lets you add the missing ones.
For example, the dialog box below shows the fields that could be added to the *Fees* layout shown on p. 113.

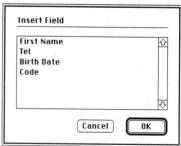

114

Layout: Info, Slide, Tab

In the *Layout Info* dialog box, you can choose to set records in columns, and slide objects to remove space between data when printing.

A well-thought-out *Tab Order* makes the database more comfortable for heavy users.

COLUMNS

Labels are set in columns by default. You can also set other types of records in columns. This is different from a Columnar layout, where *fields* are set in columns inside every record. *Across* means that record n+1 is to the right of record n or at the beginning of the next line. *Down* puts record n+1 under record n, or at the top of the next column.

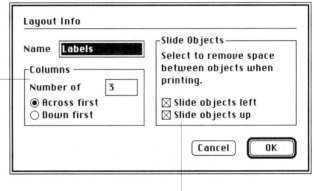

SLIDE OBJECTS

The first picture at left shows the *Labels* layout. A long address needs two lines.

The second picture shows a label with a short address. If the *Slide objects* option is not checked, the label prints as is.

As the "sliding" is not visible on screen, the third picture does not show a screen capture like the preceding ones, but a printed label: the *City* and *Code* fields slide up, the *Code* field slides left. Field labels would also slide.

The option is checked by default for Labels layouts.

TAB ORDER

The order in the Field List is the chronological field creation order. The default *Tab Order* is left-to-right and top-to-bottom.

This example shows that the program chooses to put a date field before the others.

To put *Birth Date* after *Name* and *First Name*, you should move *Birth Date, Address, City* and *Tel* left, then right again.

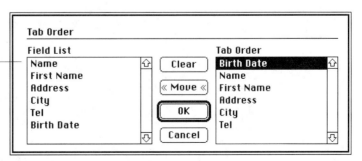

DATABASE MENUS

When a field name is selected in the *Define Fields* dialog box (for example, just after it is created), the *Options* button becomes available. Double-clicking the field name or clicking the button displays the *Entry Options* dialog box below.

AUTO ENTRY

If the data "Tokyo" is chosen as Auto Entry for the *City* field, the field for a new record reads "Tokyo"—a suggestion which can be replaced by another word. Note that data for a number or date field must be a number or date.

The *Serial number* option lets you number the records (useful if you ever want to "unsort" them). The field must be a number field. Default *next value* (for next new record) and *increment* are 1.

VARIABLE AUTO ENTRY

A field with *Creation Date* or *Time* as auto entry lets you know when the record was created; a field with *Modified Date* or *Time* indicates when it was changed. *Creator* and *Modifier Name* refer to the name of your Macintosh in System 7's Sharing Setup feature.

Creation Date
Creation Time
Modified Date
Modified Time
✓ Creator Name
Modifier Name

PRE-DEFINED LIST

When you check *Pre-defined list*, the *Edit List...* button becomes available. See opposite page.

Entry Options for Text Field "Fees in"

Auto Entry
- No auto entry
- Data
- Variable — Creator Name ▼
- Serial number
  - next value
  - increment

Input List
- Pre-defined list — Edit List...
- Only values from list

Verification
Verify field value is:
- Not empty
- Unique
- Range
  - from
  - to

Cancel   OK

Field First Name is defined to require a value. Allow this field to be empty?

No   Yes

VERIFICATION

Suppose that you check the *Not empty* option for the field *First Name*. When someone activates record A, then activates another record without entering data into field *First Name* of record A, the alert box at left appears.

Unique means: data not entered into this field in another record. This lets you avoid, for example, to create two different records for one customer. Restricting values to a range is possible only for number, date and time fields.

116

Layout: Field Options

A *Pre-defined Input List* saves a lot of time if you must often enter data belonging to a well-defined set into a field.

In the very simple example below, the list shows currency symbols. It is useful because some of them may be hard to find on the keyboard.

You might create such a list for complicated names or addresses, a series of bank account numbers, etc.

CREATE THE LIST

Clicking the *Edit List...* button (see opposite page) displays this dialog box.
As in several other Database dialog boxes, the *Create* button lets you build the list.
Click *Done* when you're satisfied with it.

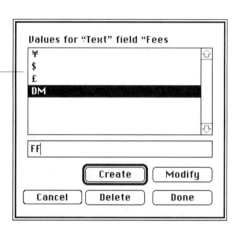

POP-UP LIST

The list appears when you activate the *Fees in* field by pressing the Tab key or by clicking.
You choose an item by double-clicking it or by selecting it and pressing the Return or Enter key. The item appears inside the field and the list vanishes.

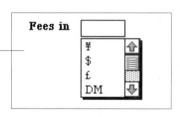

ONLY VALUES FROM LIST

When the *Only values from list* option is checked (see opposite page), trying to enter other data into the field displays this alert box.

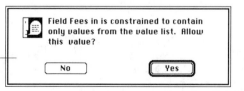

DATABASE MENUS

Sorting is a very powerful computer feature. While it may be considered a non-essential feature for spreadsheet programs, it is a central one for databases.

Most of the commands of this important menu exist as buttons on the default Database palette.

SHOW ALL

Records can be hidden because some have been "found," or because a **Hide** command has been chosen. **Show All Records** displays the whole database again.

GO TO RECORD

See p. 102.

SORT RECORDS

See below.

NAME, FIRST NAME

You should not enter "Caroline Smith" into a name field if you know that you may have to sort the records by name. Either write "Smith, Caroline" or create separate fields for first name and last name.

Separate fields was the choice of the Einstein school, as small children in the same class are often sorted by first name.

HIDE SELECTED

To select several consecutive records, click outside of fields and drag, or Shift-click each record.

To select non-consecutive records, Command-click them. You might hide selected or unselected records to make the database easier to use.

MATCH RECORDS

See opposite page.

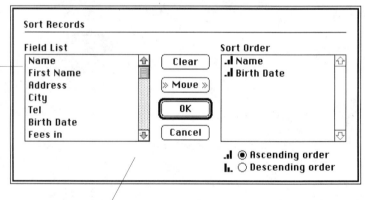

SORT

This is quite similar to a Spreadsheet sort (see p. 94), with fields acting as "keys" instead of cells.

In this example, the records will be sorted by name, and the children belonging to a family will be sorted from the eldest to the youngest.

SHORTCUTS

Second row: Sort ascending, descending; Sort again; Show records that match values, that do not match values, less than value, more than value; New record; Show all records; Hide selected.

The **Match Records...** command is a kind of cousin of the Find feature.

Choosing this command displays the Calculation dialog box, where you create a formula with the field names, operators, and functions. Records which fit the formula are selected. In the example below, two records matching a birthday formula are selected in this manner.

If you want to hide the other records and bring the matching ones together, as is done in Find mode, you should choose the **Hide Unselected** command.

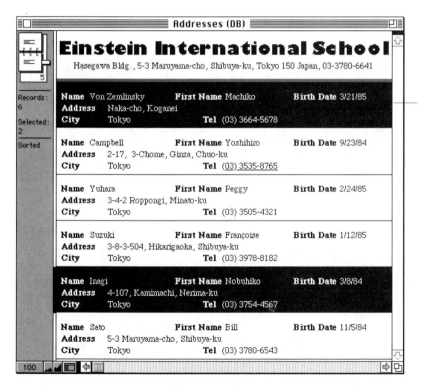

BIRTHDAY

The formula *Month('Birth Date')=3* selects the records of all the children born in March, for whom the formula is TRUE. This can't be done with the Find feature. The formula must include an operator like =, >, ≥, <,≤, or a "logical" function like AND, NOT, or ISNUMBER, which return TRUE or FALSE as a value. Matching records are the ones where TRUE is returned.
See logical functions on pp. 142 to 144.

Communications

While the other ClarisWorks modes can be combined in various ways, *Communications* is a stand-alone mode, which lets you exchange data with other computers via modems and phone lines.

You can skip this section if:

1) You work with an isolated Macintosh computer, with no links to the outside world.

2) You are linked via modem with an online service, such as Applelink, eWorld, America Online or Compuserve, that sent you its own communication program, and you are not interested in other types of data exchange.

3) You communicate via modem and *PowerTalk Direct Dialup Mail* with other System 7 Pro Macs (see p. 26).

COMMUNICATIONS

When you open a new Communications document, you see an empty window similar to the one below.

The contents of a Communications window do not act in a polite Macintosh way. The pointer is a blinking horizontal dash, and overflowing text spills from the *Terminal area* (bottom part of the window) into a special container called the *Scrollback Pane* or *Log Window* (top part of the window).

FILE
You can save and name a Communications document, i.e. its settings and contents. You can also save its settings by saving the document as ClarisWorks Stationery.

EDIT
The **Edit** menu lets you copy/cut and paste the contents of the Terminal area and Scrollback pane. See the Communications *Preferences* dialog box below.

STATUS AREA
This gray bar is called the *Status Area*. The *Connection Clock* at left monitors connection time (remember: time is money!). Clicking the clock resets it to zero. Choosing **Hide Tools** in the **View** menu hides the Status Area.

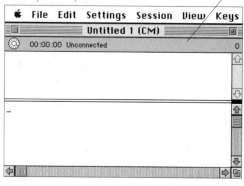

SCROLLBACK
The number of lines in the Scrollback is displayed at the right of the Status Area. In this example, it is 0. The Scrollback is hidden by default.

PHONE BUTTON
The Phone button displays a pop-up menu with the entries of your Phone Book. Choose one to connect.

PREFERENCES
This picture shows the default options. You can limit the Scrollback to a number of lines or kilobytes, and save its screens if your Online service clears them automatically. Data captured as *Screen* is "Text only," whereas *Port* includes some formatting. You can connect automatically when you open the document, or wait for an incoming connection. The *Connection, Terminal* and *File Transfer* pop-up menus let you change default Settings for new documents. See following pages.

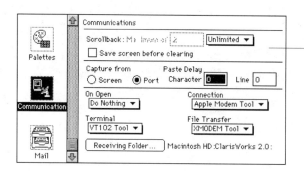

Settings: Connection

The golden rule here is: Stick with the default settings unless you know precisely what to replace them with.

CONNECTION
See below.

FILE TRANSFER
See p. 125.

SHOW SCROLLBACK
This command lets you show or hide the Scrollback. You can also drag the window's pane tool.

METHOD
Choose **Serial Tool** instead of **Apple Modem Tool** in the pop-up menu if you connect directly to another Mac (e.g., Powerbook to desktop Mac) with a cable.

PHONE NUMBER
The number entered here will be called when you choose the **Open Connection** command in the **Session** menu.
Using a phone book bypasses this process completely. See below.

PHONE BOOK
The **Phone Book...** command opens the dialog box at far right. Clicking **New** or **Edit**, or choosing **Edit Phone Book...** in the phone button pop-up menu (see opposite page) displays the dialog box at right, where you actually enter numbers and names.
If you need to dial a 9 or other number for an outside line, put a comma after it for a 2-second pause, or more commas for a longer pause. Dashes and spaces are allowed to make numbers easier to read, e.g. 9,,456-78-90.

TERMINAL
See p. 124.

INFO
Info about the current settings.

PHONE BOOK
See below.

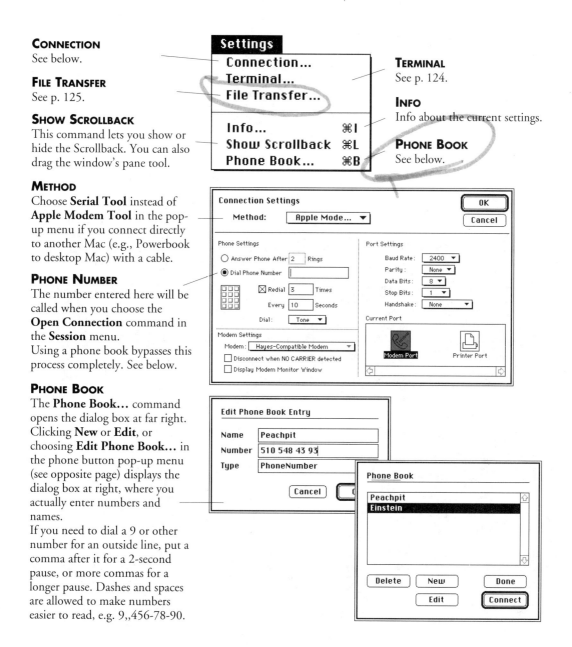

123

COMMUNICATION

In Communications mode, the Macintosh "emulates" a standard data transfer terminal. The default terminal is called VT102, but you can switch to TTY emulation if needed. The "Status Bar" mentioned below, which you can display inside the document window, emulates the status lights of a VT102 terminal.

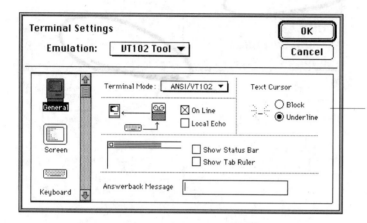

GENERAL SETTINGS
This dialog box changes when you click one of the icons at left, or when you choose TTY Tool instead of VT102 Tool.

It takes two parties to communicate. You may have to change some of the *General* settings at the request of the other party.

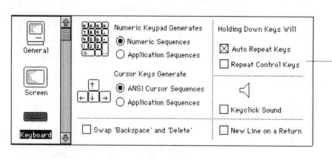

KEYBOARD SETTINGS
You may have to modify these if the other party prefers Digital Equipment keyboard sequences to VT102 "ANSI" sequences.

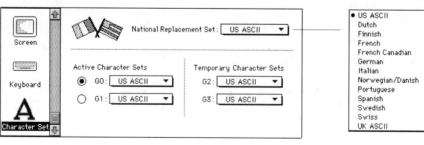

Computer communication usually means transmitting text messages that you enter into the p. 122 window, but you can also send and receive files.

The default *XModem* file transfer protocol lets you transmit any Macintosh file to another Macintosh computer by the *MacBinary* method.

Several methods and protocols exist in the Communications industry. If you fail to transmit a file, you can try switching the method from *MacBinary* to *Straight XModem* or *XModem Text*, or switch protocol from *XModem* to *Text Tool*.

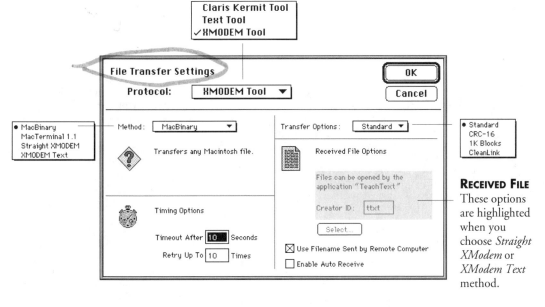

RECEIVED FILE These options are highlighted when you choose *Straight XModem* or *XModem Text* method.

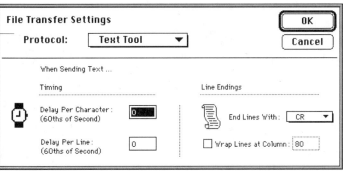

TEXT TOOL The dialog box changes to this box when the Text Tool protocol is chosen.

COMMUNICATION

After you have accepted or changed the default settings, this menu lets you begin communicating.

When you choose the **Open Connection** command, the other party's number is dialed. You can't access the document window and the Communications menus; a status window appears on the screen and tells you what's going on.

As soon as the connection is established, you can click into the document window to activate it, and try sending/receiving data or Macintosh files.

If you are connecting to an online service, you'll be asked for your name and password, etc. Just answer the questions that appear on the screen.

SEND/RECEIVE FILES

These commands are available only when you are connected.
See opposite page.

OFF TOP

This is another name for the Scrollback.
If you don't need to save incoming data at all, uncheck this command.
Clear Saved lines means *Clear the Scrollback.*

SAVE/CLEAR

Save Current Screen moves the terminal area data into the Scrollback (but it is not really saved until you choose the **Save** command in the **File** menu).
When data is saved, you can **Clear Screen** (meaning: terminal area).

SEND BREAK

To get remote system to respond, a break signal is sent.

Session
Open Connection ⇧⌘O
Wait For Connection ⇧⌘W
Send File...
Send Batch...
Receive File...
Capture To File...
✓ Save Lines Off Top ⌘T
Clear Saved Lines
Save Current Screen
Clear Screen
Reset Connection
Reset Terminal
Send Break

OPEN/WAIT

When you choose **Open Connection**, the number entered in *Connection Settings* is dialed. If no number is entered, you are prompted for a number. You can also connect directly by choosing a number in your Phone Book.
If you are expecting another party to initiate the connection, choose **Wait for Connection**.

CAPTURE TO FILE

This opens a Save-type dialog box. *Captured* incoming data is saved as a text-only Claris-Works document if *Screen* is checked in the Preferences dialog box; this is the default option. When *Port* is checked, data is saved in binary mode and may or may not be read by ClarisWorks or other programs.
When possible, sending data as Macintosh files is safer.

RESET

When things go wrong, you can try resetting the Connection or the Terminal.

126

Session, Keys, Shortcuts

Exchanging files with a remote computer over phone lines can be costly when the files are big. Compression programs (like Compact Pro, etc.) help a lot.

You can work while files are being transferred; the Macintosh beeps when the process is over.

FILE TRANSFER

Choosing the **Send File...** command displays an Open-type dialog box that lets you select the file you want to send.

When you click the *Send* button in this first dialog box, the *File Transfer Status* box at right appears.

A similar box appears when you are on the receiving end and choose the **Receive File...** command.

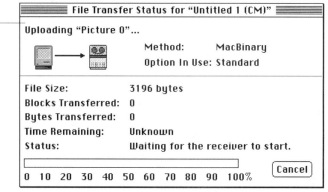

KEYS

The **Keypad** and **Cursor** submenus are part of the VT102 terminal emulation. You get the same VT102 commands by using the keyboard keys.

The **No Scroll** command is highlighted only when the "XOn/XOff Handshaking" option is chosen in the *Connection Settings* dialog box.

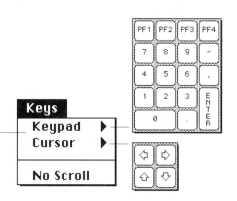

COMMUNICATIONS SHORTCUTS

Five buttons at right:
Open & Close connection,
Wait for connection,
Send & Receive a file.

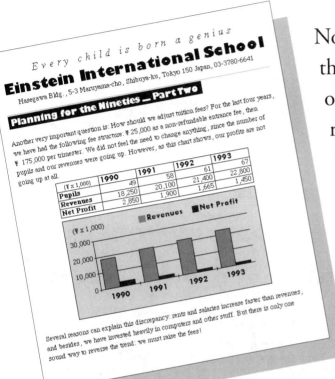

Now that you understand the various modules of ClarisWorks, you are ready to discover how they interact. Herein lies ClarisWorks' superiority over other so-called *Integrated Software.*

Right in the middle of a text document, you can create Spreadsheet mode tables and charts, or Draw and Paint mode pictures.

You can write a letter in Text mode, then send it to a list of prospects kept in a Database document—with personalized "Dear Mrs. Johnson" entries.

You can try *DeskTop Publishing (DTP)* by combining pictures and text in a Draw mode document.

EXAMPLES

The three examples given in the following pages show how to get extra power by combining several ClarisWorks modes.

In the first example, a table and a chart are added to a Text document by creating two "frames" belonging to the Spreadsheet mode. This is a fantastic table-generating feature, much superior to what dedicated word processing programs can do.

TEXT FRAME
"Planning for the Nineties—Part Two" is a Text object inside a "frame." Such a frame is created by Option-dragging the Text tool. As an object, it can be filled with a color.

OPTION-SPACE
This has nothing to do with frames and tables, but it is very important: To avoid splitting ¥ 175,000, you should type ¥-Option-space-175,000.

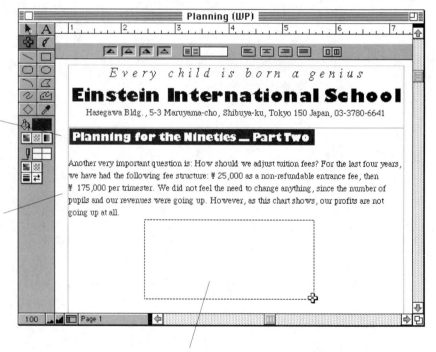

Every child is born a genius

Einstein International School

Hasegawa Bldg., 5-3 Maruyama-cho, Shibuya-ku, Tokyo 150 Japan, 03-3780-6641

Planning for the Nineties — Part Two

Another very important question is: How should we adjust tuition fees? For the last four years, we have had the following fee structure: ¥ 25,000 as a non-refundable entrance fee, then ¥ 175,000 per trimester. We did not feel the need to change anything, since the number of pupils and our revenues were going up. However, as this chart shows, our profits are not going up at all.

SPREADSHEET FRAME
To create a "frame," you must first show the tools by clicking the *Show* icon at the bottom of the window. Then select the Spreadsheet tool and drag.

The frame will contain part of a spreadsheet, but it is also an object which can be resized.

Thus, you shouldn't worry if you don't drag as precisely as you'd like.

Tables: Frame

As soon as you finish dragging with the Spreadsheet tool, you see part of a default spreadsheet, with one-inch wide columns, etc. Spreadsheet mode is on, with regular spreadsheet functions and menus.

DATA ENTRY BAR

The Spreadsheet mode Data Entry bar appears above the Text mode ruler (which you might hide to gain space).

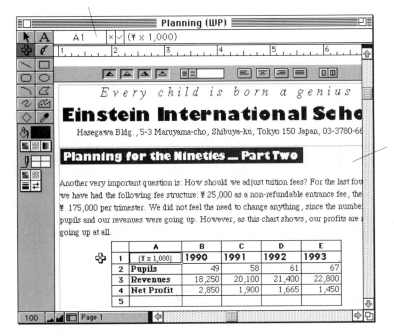

SPREADSHEET

The program displays as many one-inch columns and 14 pt rows as the frame will contain.

If you want more or fewer columns/rows, select the Arrow tool and click the frame. It becomes an object, which you can resize by dragging its handles.

Here, columns B to E have been narrowed, fonts and styles have been changed, etc. Common sense says: draw as large a frame as you can at first, then fill up cells and resize rows and columns; when you're happy with your table, use the Arrow tool to hide empty columns and rows.

OPEN FRAME

The **Open Frame** command of the Spreadsheet **View** menu displays a second window with a "view" of the complete spreadsheet. The data are the same as inside the table, but you are not limited to the frame size, which can be quite useful.

EXAMPLES

Making a chart follows the method explained on pp. 86-89. The chart is not locked inside the spreadsheet frame, but it is a separate object. At this stage, it is still "linked" to the spreadsheet: if you change data or formats in the spreadsheet frame, the chart reflects the changes.

TEXT MODE

This is a Text document. The spreadsheet and the chart do not really belong to it yet. If you type at the end of the text, what you type will actually go *behind* the frames.

DRAW MODE

When you click inside the text, you see an Insertion Point and Text menus.
When you click inside the table, you see a Crossbar Pointer and Spreadsheet menus.
When the Arrow Pointer is selected, the menu bar shows Draw menus.

SPREADSHEET MODE

The *Pupils* row has been moved out of the way, as rows 1, 2, and 3 must be selected together for chart-making.

CHART

A default bar chart.
See a chart with Draw mode add-ons on the opposite page.
The chart sits inside its own frame.
The handles can be dragged with the Arrow Pointer so that both frames have the same width.

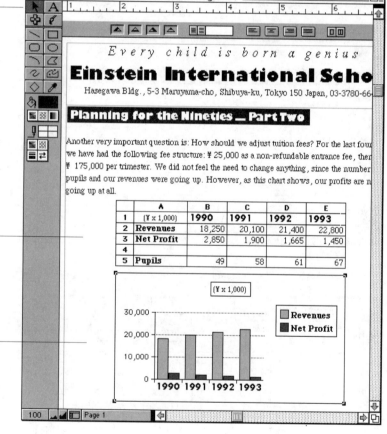

Tables: Cut and Paste

If you want a frame to belong to a Text document, cut it and paste it at the Insertion Point. It then becomes a character and moves with the paragraph it belongs to when you edit the text.

In some cases—for instance, if you make an ad or a poster—this step may not be necessary. You can leave the text and the frames separate, the way they are on the opposite page.

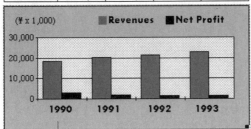

Every child is born a genius

Einstein International School

Hasegawa Bldg., 5-3 Maruyama-cho, Shibuya-ku, Tokyo 150 Japan, 03-3780-6641

Planning for the Nineties — Part Two

Another very important question is: How should we adjust tuition fees? For the last four years, we have had the following fee structure: ¥ 25,000 as a non-refundable entrance fee, then ¥ 175,000 per trimester. We did not feel the need to change anything, since the number of pupils and our revenues were going up. However, as this chart shows, our profits are not going up at all.

(¥ x 1,000)	1990	1991	1992	1993
Pupils	49	58	61	67
Revenues	18,250	20,100	21,400	22,800
Net Profit	2,850	1,900	1,665	1,450

Several reasons can explain this discrepancy: rents and salaries increase faster than revenues, and besides, we have invested heavily in computers and other stuff. But there is only one sound way to reverse the trend: we must raise the fees!

HEADER
If you want a Text object like *Planning for the Nineties—Part Two* to appear on every page, you should select it with the Arrow tool and cut it, then paste it after the Insertion Point inside the Header.

CHARACTER
The frame is selected with the Arrow tool and cut. Then the Return key is pressed after "at all," to create a new paragraph. Pasting the frame-object defines it as a Text character. The Return key is pressed again, then the chart is also cut and pasted. Both objects are thus paragraphs, which can be centered as they are here.

ONE HANDLE
When selected by a click, an object inside a text only has one handle, at bottom right.

MODIFY
Before the frame is cut, a **Modify Frame…** command in the **Options** menu of the Draw mode lets you remove the row and column Headers. When the table has become a character, you can still do it with the **Display…** command of the Spreadsheet mode **Options** menu. This is not exactly the same chart as on the opposite page. The spreadsheet selection did not include column A; thus, title and legends can be Text objects (created by Option-dragging with the Text tool) grouped with the Chart object.

EXAMPLES

To appreciate how easy it is to create form letters or similar documents with ClarisWorks, you should try the mail merge function of a dedicated word processing program (let's say, Microsoft Word...) and compare!

What makes it so easy is that data is already neatly organized inside a Database mode document. All you have to do to start the process is to open the Text document (i.e. the form letter) and the Database document together.

INSERTION POINT
Put the Insertion Point where you want data from a certain field to appear.
Here, we want to insert the contents of the *Name* field of the Database, so that this line reads, "The Campbell family."

DATABASE
Whatever the displayed layout, the program is ready to consider all the existing fields, i.e. the *Define Fields* list.

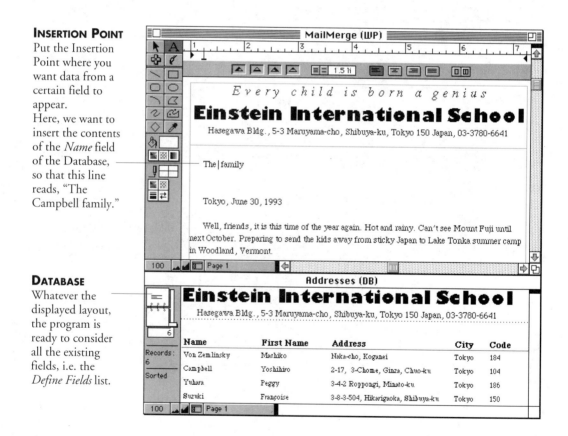

You are allowed to open several Database documents at once, but only one "merge" (Text) document.

Choosing the **Mail Merge...** command in the **File** menu displays the *Select Data* dialog box. Clicking OK displays the *Mail Merge* palette, which stays in front of your Text document while you insert fields.

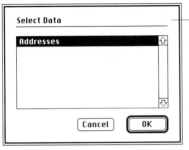

SELECT DATA

If you have opened several Database documents, you can select one here.

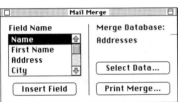

PALETTE

Select a field name and click *Insert Field* to enter it after the Insertion Point.

Click *Print Merge* to start the printing.

INSERT FIELDS

The field name appears after the Insertion Point between delimiters called "double angle brackets." If you want to get («) without clicking field names on the palette, press Option-\;
(») is Option-Shift-\.
When the *Print Merge...* button of the palette is clicked, as many letters as there are records in the database are printed:
the first one is addressed to Campbell, the second one to Von Zemlinsky, etc.

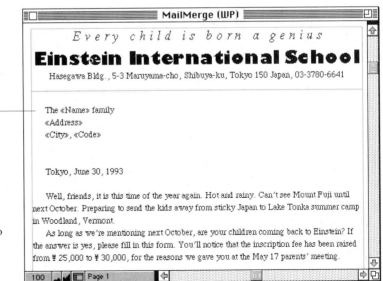

Every child is born a genius

Einstein International School

Hasegawa Bldg., 5-3 Maruyama-cho, Shibuya-ku, Tokyo 150 Japan, 03-3780-6641

The «Name» family
«Address»
«City», «Code»

Tokyo, June 30, 1993

Well, friends, it is this time of the year again. Hot and rainy. Can't see Mount Fuji until next October. Preparing to send the kids away from sticky Japan to Lake Tonka summer camp in Woodland, Vermont.

As long as we're mentioning next October, are your children coming back to Einstein? If the answer is yes, please fill in this form. You'll notice that the inscription fee has been raised from ¥ 25,000 to ¥ 30,000, for the reasons we gave you at the May 17 parents' meeting.

135

EXAMPLES

The Einstein International School uses ClarisWorks to make a magazine. In the example below, several Text objects have been created inside a Draw mode document. The most recent Text object is different from the others: it is a "linked text frame." To make one, you choose **Frame Links** in the **Options** menu, select the Text tool and drag.

PAINT
This picture was drawn in Paint mode and pasted here.

FREE TEXT OBJECTS
The word Nesumi ("mouse" in Japanese) and the italic line are two different objects, so they can be moved separately.

DRAW
Although you can do rough DTP with the Text mode of ClarisWorks, starting from the Draw mode gives you more freedom to place elements wherever you wish on the page.

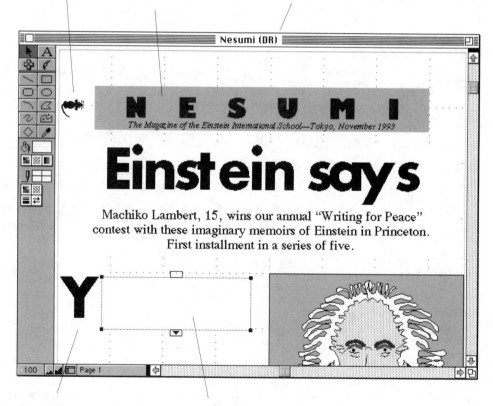

DROP CAP
This is a regular Text object.

LINKED TEXT FRAME
You must choose the Arrow tool and click on the object to see it like this.

When a linked-text-frame object is selected with the Arrow tool, a small triangle, called a "Continue indicator," appears at its bottom.

To make a new text frame that will be linked to the first one, click on the triangle. The Text tool is automatically selected, so that you can create the new linked frame by dragging.

It is usually difficult or even impossible to create the frame exactly where you'd like it. Just drag where you can: the frame is an object, which you can resize and move later. More about this on the next page.

LINK INDICATOR
The link between two frames is symbolized by a chain icon (or "Link indicator") at the bottom of the first one and at the top of the second.

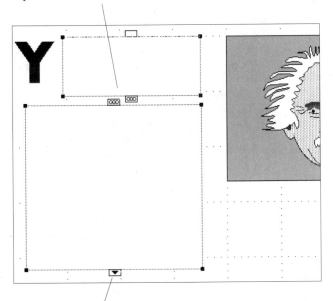

CONTINUE INDICATOR
The triangle says that this is the end of a series of linked frames.
Click on the triangle and drag to extend the series.
Next frame could be under Einstein, or on another page.
As you may remember, the **Document...** command of the **Format** menu lets you give a Draw document as many pages as you want.

TEXT OVERFLOW INDICATOR
A small crossed square at the bottom right of the last frame means that there is more text than meets the eye.
You may enlarge the frame, or create another linked frame for the text to spill into.

EXAMPLES

ClarisWorks does not promise you full DTP power. If you want to give your page a professional look, you should design it with the program's limitations in mind. You may also invent little tricks, like the Custom Ruler described below, to circumvent the limitations.

You can create form letters with Mail Merge text frames, and link Spreadsheet frames, and do many more things with ClarisWorks. By now, you should know enough to explore the program by yourself!

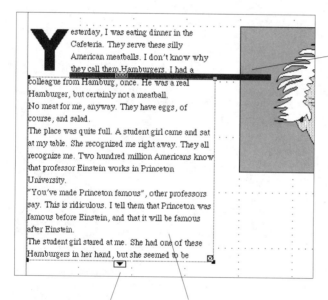

CUSTOM RULER
This gray line is a kind of custom ruler.
Adjusting its length to the width of the selected frame helps you create a similar frame under Einstein.
Its thickness is 8 pt. When you insert it between two text lines in this 10 pt interline example, you can check that there is a one pixel gap between the ruler and the text lines above and below (you may need to zoom in if your screen or eyes fail you).
When you insert the custom ruler between the last line of frame 1 and the first line of frame 2 in this example, it appears that frame 2 has not been moved up enough: there are 2 pixels below the ruler, i.e. 11 pt between the two lines instead of 10. Pressing the Up arrow key once will correct this small defect.

TEXT/DRAW MODE
On the preceding page, this frame was seen in Text mode, with no handles and no Continue indicator.
You can have a Text mode frame with no text, or a Draw mode frame with text, as above.
When things don't come out as you'd like, remember that you can try the other mode.

ONE TEXT
In the end, it looks as if there were one text (see next page). When the Insertion Point blinks inside a linked frame, choosing the **Select All** command selects the text through all the frames.
For Import/Export purposes, there is one text only.

N E S U M I

The Magazine of the Einstein International School—Tokyo, November 1993

Einstein says

Machiko Lambert, 15, wins our annual "Writing for Peace" contest with these imaginary memoirs of Einstein in Princeton. First installment in a series of five.

Yesterday, I was eating dinner in the Cafeteria. They serve these silly American meatballs. I don't know why they call them Hamburgers. I had a colleague from Hamburg, once. He was a real Hamburger, but certainly not a meatball.

No meat for me, anyway. They have eggs, of course, and salad.

The place was quite full. A student girl came and sat at my table. She recognized me right away. They all recognize me. Two hundred million Americans know that professor Einstein works in Princeton University. "You've made Princeton famous," other professors say. This is ridiculous. I tell them that Princeton was famous before Einstein, and that it will be famous after Einstein.

The student girl stared at me. She had one of these Hamburgers in her hand, but she seemed to be hesitating before biting into it.

"Are you proud of yourself?" she asked suddenly. "You killed millions of people with your atomic bomb, and now the Russians got one, too, and I bet they'll blow up the whole planet soon enough.... Let me tell you something: it would have been better if you had stayed home on the day you went and invented this stupid bomb!"

"It's not my bomb," I said.

I really hate it when they say, "your bomb." I wanted to tell her that I had never killed anybody, that the people who should have stayed home were the ones who voted for Hitler in 1933, that.... But she took her Hamburger and moved to another table. A very young girl she was, with blonde hair and nice round American cheeks.

This kind of thing happens all the time. Can't help it, I guess. I felt a little sorry for her, and also for myself, and I didn't sleep very well.

This morning, I decided that I would write a kind of letter to her. I need to explain a few things. To justify myself, and perhaps to apologize. Whether I'll give her the letter (supposing I can recognize her) is something I'll have to decide later.

Appendix

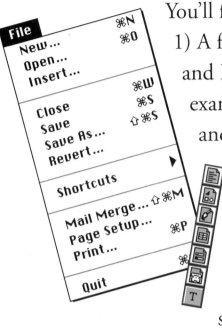

You'll find in this appendix:

1) A full list of ClarisWorks Spreadsheet and Database *Functions*. See also examples of function usage on pp. 84 and 93 (Spreadsheet mode); on pp. 110 and 113 (Database mode).

2) All the menus for the various modes.

3) A full list of the "available" shortcuts which you can access through the *Edit Shortcuts* dialog box (see p. 22).

APPENDIX

Unless indicated otherwise, functions can be used both in Spreadsheet *(SS)* formulas and in Database *(DB)* Calculation field formulas. They "return" a number or a string of characters.

Functions need one or several *arguments,* which can be numbers, text, cell addresses, field names, or other functions.

For example, **Abs** *(Number)* means that you can write Abs (Rate), where "Rate" is the name of a Database Number field. **Sum** *(Number1,Number2)* means you can write Sum (C4,C5), where C4 and C5 are cell addresses.

Abs *(Number)*
Absolute value of *Number.*
Acos *(Number)*
Arccosine (in radians) of *Number.*
Alert *(Message)* – SS only.
Displays a message in a dialog box. *Message* can be a text between quotes or a cell address or an expression. Used as argument of the function **If**.
And *(Number1,Number2,…)*
Returns True if all the arguments are ≠0, False if one argument =0.
Asin *(Number)*
Arcsine of *Number.*
Atan *(Number)*
Arctangent of *Number.*
Atan2 *(X-Number,Y-Number)*
Polar angle (in radians) of a point, given its coordinates.
Average *(Number1,Number2,…)*
The arguments can be numbers, cell addresses, or a cell range: Average (B1..C4) is legitimate.
Beep *( )*
Plays the alert sound of the Macintosh. Used as argument of the function **If**.
Char *(Number)*
Returns the ASCII character which corresponds to *Number.*
Choose *(N, Value1, Value2,…)*
Returns the Nth value in the list.

N can be a number or a cell address, etc.
Code *(Text)*
Returns the ASCII number of the first character of *Text.*
Column *({CellAddress})* – SS only.
Returns the column number of *CellAddress.* If this function is entered into a cell, it takes the address of the cell as argument if no other argument is given.
Concat *(Text1,Text2,…)*
Concatenates (puts together) strings of text.
Cos *(AngleInRadians)*
Cosine of *AngleInRadians.*
Count *(Value1, Value2,…)*
Returns the number of arguments.
Count2 *(Value1, Value2,…)*
Returns the number of occurences of *Value1* in the list of arguments which follows.
Date *(Year,Month,Day,)*
Year, Month and *Day* are numbers. Returns the Macintosh number for the date, which measures the time elapsed since 1/1/1904 (a conventional Macintosh "day one") to the current date.

DateToText *(DateNumber, {Format})*
DateNumber is the Macintosh number for a date (see above) or a Date field. The function returns the date as a string of text. Format is a number from 0 to 4. When it is 0 (or absent), the string of text looks like 4/14/92. See the five formats on p. 91.
Day *(DateNumber)*
Returns the day corresponding to *DateNumber* as a number between 1 and 31.
DateNumber can't be a string of numbers like 05/11/1993, but should be a Macintosh number for a date (see **Date**, above). Since you can use a function as a parameter, the expression Day (TextToDate ("05/11/1993")) is legitimate, and returns the number 11.
DayName *(DayNumber)*
DayNumber is a number between 1 and 7. The function returns a name, from Sunday (1) to Saturday (7).
DayOfYear *(DateNumber)*
Number of days from the beginning of year until the current date.

Degrees *(AngleInRadians)*
Converts radians to degrees.
Error *( )*
Returns the value #ERROR!
Used as argument of the function
If.
Exact *(Text1, Text2)*
Returns True if *Text1* and *Text2*
are identical. The comparison is
case-sensitive: ABC is different
from abc.
Exp *(Number)*
Exponential of *Number*.
Fact *(Number)*
Factorial of *Number*.
Find *(Text1, Text2, {OffsetNumber})*
Starts from the beginning of
Text2 or from the beginning of
Text2 + *OffsetNumber*, and
returns the rank of the first
character of *Text1*—supposing
Text1 is to be found somewhere
inside *Text2*.
This is case sensitive.
Example:
Find ("Mac","Nice Machine!")
returns 6, because M is the sixth
character of "Nice Machine!"
Frac *(Number)*
Returns the fractional (decimal)
part of *Number*. For example,
Frac (4.567) is 0.567.
FV *(InterestRate, NbOfPeriods,
PaymentPerPeriod, {PresentValue},
{Type})*
Returns the future value of an
investment. *Type* is 0 for payment
at end of period, 1 for payment at
start of period. If there is no
PresentValue and no *Type*, the
program sets them to 0.

HLookUp *(Value, CellRange,
RowOffset, {Method})* – SS only.
When *Method* is absent or is 1,
this function searches the top row
of a range of cells with increasing
values, from left to right, until it
finds the greatest entry ≤*Value*. It
then adds *RowOffset* to the row
number and returns the value of
the found cell. When *Method* is -
1, the range should decrease from
left to right, and the function
finds the smallest entry ≥*Value*.
When Method is 0, the function
looks for an entry equal to *Value*.
Hour *(TimeNumber)*
TimeNumber is a number
between 0 and 1, or the decimal
part of a Date number. The
function considers the argument
as a fraction of the day, and
returns a number between 0 and
23.
If *(Test, Result1, Result2)*
When *Test* is true or ≠0, the
function evaluates the expression
Result1 and returns it; if *Test* is
false or =0, the evaluation of
Result2 is returned.
Example:
If (price>12,"No","Yes") returns
No when the price is too high.
The *Test* expression can include
the logical operators and/or/not,
the *Result1* and *Result2*
expressions can include functions
like **Error** *( )* or nested ifs:
If (price>12 and sky=blue,
0,if(curr="$",0,1)).

Index *(CellRange, RowOffset,
ColumnOffset)* – SS only.
Starts from the top left of
CellRange, moves *RowOffset* rows
downward and *ColumnOffset*
columns rightward, and returns
the value of the found cell.
Int *(Number)*
Integer part of number. Int(3.9)
returns 3.
IRR *(RangeOfCells, {Guess})* – SS
only. Calculates an Internal Rate
of Return by repeated approxim-
ations, starting from Guess, or
from 10% if no *Guess* is given.
IsBlank *(Value)*
Returns True if *Value* is empty,
False if not. A cell or field is not
empty if it contains 0.
IsError *(Value, {ErrorType})*
Returns True when *Value* is not a
legitimate expression. *ErrorType* is
one of ten error types, like #N/A!
or #ARG! (Invalid Argument).
IsLogical *(Value)* – SS only.
Returns True if *Value* is a
Boolean (i.e., logical) expression,
False if not. An expression is
Boolean when it can be
considered True or False,
like a<b.
IsNA *(Value)*
Returns True if *Value* is #N/A!
IsNumber *(Value)*
Returns True if *Value* is a
number.
IsText *(Value)*
Returns True if *Value* is a text.
Left *(Text, Number)*
Returns the *Number* first
characters of *Text*.

APPENDIX

Len *(Text)*
Number of characters in Text, including spaces.

Ln *(Number)*
Base-e logarithm of *Number.*

Log *(Number, {Base})*
Unless you give a *Base*, returns Base-10 logarithm of *Number.*

Log10 *(Number)*
Base-10 logarithm of *Number.*

LookUp *(Value,CellRange1, CellRange2,{Method})* – SS only.
The function looks for the greatest entry ≤*Value* through *CellRange1* (which should have increasing values), moving from left to right, row after row. It returns the value of the cell similarly located in *CellRange2*.
See **HLookUp** for an explanation of *Method.*

Lower *(Text)*
Converts *Text* to lowercase.

Macro *("Name1", {Name2,…})*
Executes one or several macro(s). To be used as argument of the **If** function.

Match *(Value, CellRange,{Method})* – SS only.
Looks for the greatest entry ≤*Value* through *CellRange* (which should have increasing values), moving from left to right, row after row; returns the number of cells from the first (upper-left) one to the found cell.
See **HLookUp** for an explanation of *Method.*

Max *(Number1,Number2,…)*
Returns the highest value in the list of arguments.

Mid *(Text,Number1,Number2)*
Returns *Number2* letters of *Text*, starting at letter *Number1.*
Example: Mid ("Apple",3,2*)* returns pl.

Min *(Number1,Number2,…)*
Returns the lowest value in the list of arguments.

Minute *(TimeNumber)*
TimeNumber is a number between 0 and 1, or the decimal part of a Date number. The function considers the argument as a fraction of the day, and returns the number of minutes (between 0 and 59) after the hour.

MIRR *(SafeRate,RiskRate, Value1,Value2,…)*
Modified Internal Rate of Return. The two first parameters can be cells formatted as percents, and the list of values can be replaced by a range of cells.

Mod *(Number,Divisor)*
Returns the remainder of the division of number by divisor. Example: Mod (27,5) returns 2.

Month *(DateNumber)*
The month corresponding to *DateNumber* is returned as a number between 1 and 12.

MonthName *(Number)*
The argument is a number between 1 and 12.

NA *( )*
Returns the value #N/A! (meaning not available). Used as argument of the function **If**.

Not *(BooleanExpression)*
Returns True if *BooleanExpression* is False.

Now *( )*
Takes as argument the date given by the Macintosh clock and returns the Date number—which does appear as a date in a Date field.

NPER *(InterestRate,PaymentPer-Period,PresentValue,{FutureValue}, {Type})*
Returns the number of periods. If no *FutureValue* and *Type* are given, the program sets them to 0.

NPV *(InterestRate, Payment1, Payment2,…)*
Returns the Net Present Value. The list of payments can be replaced by a range of cells.

NumToText *(Number)*
Returns a string of text similar to the contents of *Number*, to be used by a text function. Example: Len (NumToText (1992)) returns 4.

Or *(Number1,Number2,…)*
Returns True if one of the numbers is ≠0, False if all the arguments are =0.

Pi *( )*
Returns 3.1415926535…

PMT *(InterestRate,NumberOf Periods,PresentValue,{FutureValue}, {Type})*
Returns the payment per period.

Product *(Number1,Number2,…)*
Multiplies the numbers.

Proper *(Text)*
Converts the first letter of each word in text to uppercase and the others to lowercase. Example: Proper ("APPLE macintosh") returns Apple Macintosh.

Functions

PV
(InterestRate,NumberOfPeriods, Payment,{FutureValue},{Type})
Returns the present value of an investment.

Radians *(AngleInDegrees)*
Converts degrees to radians.

Rand *({Number})*
Rand ( ) returns a random number between 0 and 1 (but not 0 or 1).
Rand (3) returns 1, 2 or 3. It is thus different from Rand ( )*3.

Rate *(FutureValue,PresentValue, NumberOfPayments)*
Returns the rate per period.

Replace *(Text,Number1, Number2,String)*
Deletes *Number2* characters of *Text*, starting at character *Number1*, inserts *String* in their place. Example: If field Phone contains numbers like 33-0-48-87-28-27 and the phone company replaces 0 with 75, you could create a field NewPhone with the formula Replace (Phone,4,1,"75").

Rept *(Text,Number)*
Text is repeated *Number* times.

Right *(Text,Number)*
See **Left**.

Round *(Number1,Number2)*
Rounds *Number1* to *Number2* places. Examples: Round (3.187,2) returns 3.19; Round (225,-2) returns 200.

Row *({CellAddress})* – SS only.
See **Column**.

Second *(TimeNumber)*
TimeNumber is a number

between 0 and 1, or the decimal part of a Date number. The function considers the argument as a fraction of the day, and returns the number of seconds (between 0 and 59) after the minute.

Sign *(Number)*
Returns -1, 0 or 1 according to the sign of *Number*.

Sin *(AngleInRadians)*
Sine of angle.

Sqrt *(Number)*
Square root of *Number*.

StDev *(Number1,Number2,…)*
Standard deviation of a list of numbers.

Sum *(Number1,Number2,…)*
Adds the numbers.

Tan *(AngleInRadians)*
Tangent of angle.

TextToDate *(DateAsText)*
Converts a text date, written in any of the five date formats, into a Date number. Use this function to provide a parameter for a date function.

TextToNum *(Text)*
Deletes all non-numeric characters from text and returns a number. Example: TextToNum ("2 a 2") returns 22.

TextToTime *(TimeAsText)*
Converts a text time, written as 10:15 PM or as 22:15, into a number between 0 and 1, which can be recognized by a time function.

Time *(Hours,Minutes,Seconds)*
Converts three numbers (between

0 and 23, 0 and 59, 0 and 59) into a number between 0 and 1.

TimeToText *(TimeNumber, {Format})*
TimeNumber is the decimal part of a number, considered a fraction of the day. *Format* is a number, from 0 to 3. 0 is 10:15 PM, 1 is 10:15:45 PM, 2 is 22:15, 3 is 22:15:45.

Trim *(Text)*
Deletes extra spaces before, after and within *Text*. Example: Trim ("Two Spaces") returns "Two Spaces."

Trunc *(Number)*
Deletes the decimal part of *Number*. Trunc (-3.9) returns -3. This is different from **Int**: Int(-3.9) returns -4.

Type *(Value)*
Returns 1 if *Value* is empty, 2 if it is logical, 3 for a number, 4 for text.

Upper *(Text)*
Converts *Text* to uppercase.

Var *(Number1,Number2,…)*
Variance of a list of numbers.

VLookUp *(Value,CellRange, ColumnOffset, {Method})* – SS only.
See **HLookUp**.

WeekDay *(DateNumber)*
Returns the day corresponding to *DateNumber* as a number between 1 and 7.

WeekOfYear *(DateNumber)*
Returns the number of the week in the year (between 1 and 52).

Year *(DateNumber)*
Returns the year of *DateNumber*.

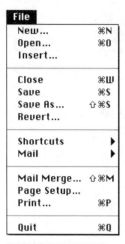

File

New...	⌘N
Open...	⌘O
Insert...	
Close	⌘W
Save	⌘S
Save As...	⇧⌘S
Revert...	
Shortcuts	▶
Mail	▶
Mail Merge...	⇧⌘M
Page Setup...	
Print...	⌘P
Quit	⌘Q

Show Shortcuts	⇧⌘K
Edit Shortcuts...	
Record Macro...	⇧⌘J
Play Macro...	
Edit Macros...	
Delete Macros...	
Macro Wait...	

Add Mailer	
Send...	
Reply	
Reply to All	
Forward	

Edit

Undo Typing	⌘Z
Cut	⌘X
Copy	⌘C
Paste	⌘V
Clear	
Select All	⌘A
Insert Date	
Insert Time	
Insert Page #	
Writing Tools	▶
Find/Change	▶
Publishing	▶
Preferences...	
Show Clipboard	

Check Document Spelling...	⌘=
Check Selection Spelling...	⇧⌘Y
Install Dictionaries...	
Auto Hyphenate	
Thesaurus...	⇧⌘Z

Find/Change...	⌘F
Find Again	⌘E
Find Selection	⇧⌘E

Create Publisher...	
Subscribe To...	
Publisher Options...	
Hide Borders	

Format

Document...	
Rulers...	
Columns...	
Paragraph...	
Tab...	
Copy Ruler	⇧⌘C
Apply Ruler	⇧⌘V
Scale Selection..	
Insert Break	
Insert Footnote	⇧⌘F
Remove Header	
Insert Footer	

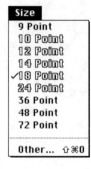

Size

9 Point	
10 Point	
12 Point	
14 Point	
✓18 Point	
24 Point	
36 Point	
48 Point	
72 Point	
Other...	⇧⌘O

	New WP
	New DR
	New PT
	New SS
	New DB
	New CM

	Open
	Save
	Insert
	Print
	Edit Shortcuts

	Record Macro
	Play Macro
	Edit Macro
	Add/Delete Mailer
	Send Letter
	Reply
	Forward Letter

	Undo
	Cut
	Copy
	Paste
	Clear

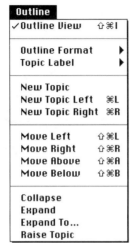

Style
- ✓Plain Text ⌘T
- **Bold** ⌘B
- *Italic* ⌘I
- Underline ⌘U
- ~~Strike Thru~~
- Outline
- Shadow
- Condense
- Extend
- Superscript ⇧⌘+
- Subscript ⇧⌘-
- Text Color ▶
- Define Styles...

Outline
- ✓Outline View ⇧⌘I
- Outline Format ▶
- Topic Label ▶
- New Topic
- New Topic Left ⌘L
- New Topic Right ⌘R
- Move Left ⇧⌘L
- Move Right ⇧⌘R
- Move Above ⇧⌘A
- Move Below ⇧⌘B
- Collapse
- Expand
- Expand To...
- Raise Topic

Outline Format submenu:
- ✓Diamond Format
- Numeric Format
- Harvard Format
- Legal Format
- Bulleted List
- Check List
- Custom Format
- Edit Custom...

Topic Label submenu:
- None
- ✓Diamond
- Bullet
- Check Box
- Harvard
- Leader
- Legal
- Letter Caps
- Letter
- Numeric
- Roman Caps
- Roman

View
- New View
- Open Frame
- ✓Page View ⇧⌘P
- Slide Show...
- Hide Tools ⇧⌘T
- Hide Rulers ⇧⌘U
- Tile Windows
- Stack Windows
- Einstein (DR)
- ✓Untitled 1 (WP)

- Spellcheck
- Auto Hyphenate
- Copy Ruler
- Apply Ruler
- Size up 1 pt
- Size down 1 pt

- Align Left
- Align Center
- Align Right
- Justified
- Superscript
- Subscript

- Plain Text
- Bold
- Italic
- Underline
- Barred
- Custom Style
- Make Table

- Stack Windows
- Tile Windows
- Show/Hide Margins
- Show/H. Page Guides
- Show/H. Invisibles

147

Draw, Paint

Edit

Undo Reshape	⌘Z
Cut	⌘X
Copy	⌘C
Paste	⌘U
Clear	
Select All	⌘A
Duplicate	⌘D
Reshape	⌘R
Smooth	⌘(
Unsmooth	⌘)
Spelling	▶
Find/Change	▶
Publishing	▶
Preferences...	
Show Clipboard	

Format

Document...	
Rulers...	
Font	▶
Size	▶
Style	▶
Text Color	▶
Alignment	▶
Spacing	▶
Insert Header	
Insert Footer	

✓Left	⌘[
Center	⌘\
Right	⌘]
Justify	⇧⌘\

✓Single Space
1-1/2 Space
Double Space

Arrange

Move Forward	⇧⌘+
Move To Front	
Move Backward	⇧⌘-
Move To Back	
Align To Grid	⌘K
Align Objects...	⇧⌘K
Rotate	⇧⌘R
Flip Horizontal	
Flip Vertical	
Group	⌘G
Ungroup	⇧⌘G
Lock	⌘H
Unlock	⇧⌘H

Options

Hide Graphics Grid	
Turn Autogrid Off	⌘Y
Edit Master Page	
Scale Selection...	
Object Size...	
Object Info...	⇧⌘I
Text Wrap...	
Patterns...	
Gradients...	
Frame Links	⌘L

Format

Document...
Rulers...
Resolution & Depth...
Font ▶
Size ▶
Style ▶
Text Color ▶
Alignment ▶
Spacing ▶
Insert Header
Insert Footer

Transform

Shear
Distort
Perspective
Free Rotate
Resize
Flip Horizontal
Flip Vertical
Rotate...
Scale Selection...
Fill
Pick Up
Invert
Blend
Tint
Lighter
Darker

Options

Turn Autogrid On	⌘Y
Grid Size...	
Brush Shape...	
Spray Can...	
Paint Mode...	
Patterns...	
Gradients...	

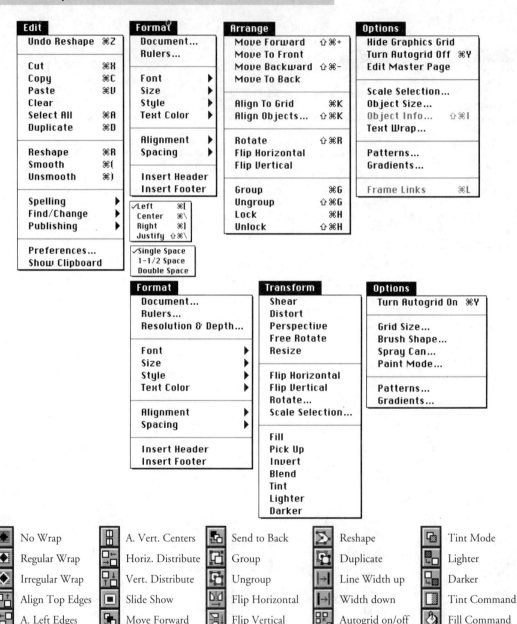

No Wrap	A. Vert. Centers	Send to Back	Reshape	Tint Mode
Regular Wrap	Horiz. Distribute	Group	Duplicate	Lighter
Irregular Wrap	Vert. Distribute	Ungroup	Line Width up	Darker
Align Top Edges	Slide Show	Flip Horizontal	Width down	Tint Command
A. Left Edges	Move Forward	Flip Vertical	Autogrid on/off	Fill Command
A. Bottom Edges	Bring to Front	Rotate 90°	Opaque Mode	Blend
A. Right Edges	Move Backward	Smooth	Transparent Mode	Invert
A. Horiz. Centers		Unsmooth		Pickup

Edit

Undo Clear	⌘Z
Cut	⌘H
Copy	⌘C
Paste	⌘U
Clear	
Select All	⌘A
Copy Format	⇧⌘C
Paste Format	⇧⌘U
Paste Special...	
Paste Function...	
Spelling	▶
Find/Change	▶
Publishing	▶
Preferences...	
Show Clipboard	

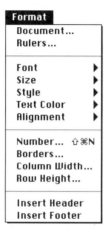

Format

Document...	
Rulers...	
Font	▶
Size	▶
Style	▶
Text Color	▶
Alignment	▶
Number...	⇧⌘N
Borders...	
Column Width...	
Row Height...	
Insert Header	
Insert Footer	

Options

Make Chart...	⌘M
Protect Cells	⌘H
Unprotect Cells	⇧⌘H
Add Page Break	
Remove Page Break	
Remove All Breaks	
Lock Title Position	
Print Range...	
Default Font...	
Display...	
Go To Cell...	⌘G

Calculate

Move...	
Fill Right	⌘R
Fill Down	⌘D
Sort...	⌘J
Insert Cells...	⇧⌘I
Delete Cells...	⇧⌘K
Calculate Now	⇧⌘=
✓Auto Calc	

	Set Print All
	Set Print Selection
	Copy Cell Format
	Paste Cell Format
Σ	Auto Sum
	Outline Border
	Left Border
	Top Border
	Right Border
	Bottom Border

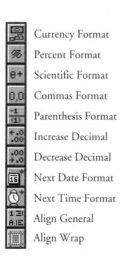

	Currency Format
%	Percent Format
e+	Scientific Format
0,0	Commas Format
-1(1)	Parenthesis Format
+.0 .00	Increase Decimal
.00 +.0	Decrease Decimal
16	Next Date Format
	Next Time Format
1 A	Align General
	Align Wrap

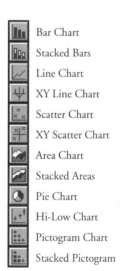

	Bar Chart
	Stacked Bars
	Line Chart
	XY Line Chart
	Scatter Chart
	XY Scatter Chart
	Area Chart
	Stacked Areas
	Pie Chart
	Hi-Low Chart
	Pictogram Chart
	Stacked Pictogram

	Show/Hide Formulas
	Show/Hide Gridlines
	Show/Hide Headers
	Show/Hide Solid Lines
	Insert Cells
	Delete Cells
	Protect Cells
	Unprotect Cells
	Auto-Size Row
	Auto-Size Column
	Auto-Calc on/off
	Calculate Now

149

Database, Communications

Edit

Can't Undo	⌘Z
Cut	⌘X
Copy	⌘C
Paste	⌘V
Clear	
Select All	⌘A
New Record	⌘R
Duplicate Record	⌘D
Copy Summaries	
Writing Tools	▶
Find/Change	▶
Publishing	▶
Preferences...	
Show Clipboard	

Layout

✓Browse	⇧⌘B
Find	⇧⌘F
Layout	⇧⌘L
New Layout...	
Delete Layout	
Layout Info...	
Tab Order...	
✓List View	
Define Fields...	⇧⌘D
Insert Field...	
Insert Part...	
✓Layout 1	⌘1
List	⌘2
Labels	⌘3
Fees	⌘4

Organize

Show All Records	⇧⌘A
Hide Selected	⌘(
Hide Unselected	⌘)
Go To Record...	⌘G
Sort Records...	⌘J
Match Records...	⌘M

Settings

Connection...	
Terminal...	
File Transfer...	
Info...	⌘I
Log Window	⌘L

Session

Open Connection	⇧⌘O
Wait for Connection	⇧⌘W
Send File...	
Receive File...	
Capture Data...	
✓Save Lines Off Top	⌘T
Clear Saved Lines	
Save Current Screen	
Clear Screen	
Reset Connection	
Reset Terminal	
Send Break	

Keys

Keypad	▶
Cursor	▶
No Scroll	

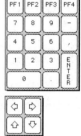

PF1	PF2	PF3	PF4
7	8	9	-
4	5	6	,
1	2	3	ENTER
0		.	

Delete Record	
New Record	
Show All Records	
Hide Selected	
Hide Unselected	

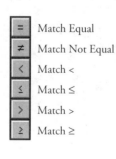

Browse Mode	
Find Mode	
Layout Mode	
Sort Ascending	
Sort Descending	
Sort Again	

=	Match Equal
≠	Match Not Equal
<	Match <
≤	Match ≤
>	Match >
≥	Match ≥

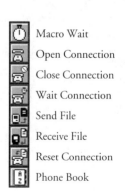

Macro Wait	
Open Connection	
Close Connection	
Wait Connection	
Send File	
Receive File	
Reset Connection	
Phone Book	

150

A

About ClarisWorks 16
Add Numbers 84
Align
    Text 12, 60
    Objects 63
    Spreadsheet 85, 91
America Online 121
Anchor Points 59
AppleLink 121
Apply 13
Arrow Tool 52, 58
Arrows 54
ATM 38
Auto Calc 92
Auto Entry 116
Autogrid 52, 61, 64, 78

B

Backspace 3, 10
Backup Copy 21
Bezigon 59
Blend 77
Book 101, 102
Borders 91
Break 37
Browse 102
Brush Editor 72
Brush Shape 72, 78
Bullets 13

C

Calculate Now 92
Capture to File 126
Cell 82
Character Styles 39
Chart
    3-D Effect 87
    Area 89
    Axis 86
    Axis Label 87

    Data Labels 86, 88
    Gallery 86, 88
    Hi-Low 89
    Labels 86
    Legends 86
    Line 88
    Pictograms 89
    Pie 88
    Scatter 88
    Series 86
    Shadow 87
    Title 86
    X-Y Line/Scatter 89
Charts 86
Circular Reference 97
Claris Translator 20
ClarisWorks 1.0 59
Clear 30
Clear (Spreadsheet) 90
Clip Art 71
Clipboard 31
Color
    Edit 55
    Fill 54
    Palette 70
    Text 38
Column Headers 82, 97
Column Width 83
Columns 12, 37
Columns (Database) 115
Communications 121
Compuserve 121
Condense 11
Connection 123, 126
Continue Indicator 137
Cover 29
Cut/Copy/Paste 31
Cut/Copy/Paste (Draw) 56

Cut/Copy/Paste (Frame) 133
Cut/Copy/Paste (Spreadsheet) 90

D

Database Mode 99
Date Format 30
Date Format (Spreadsheet) 91
Default Font 96
Define Fields 100
Define Part 101
Delete 3, 10
Delete Cells 95
Desktop 2, 21
Dictionaries 32
Display (Spreadsheet) 97
Distort 76
Divisions 61, 74
Document 36
    Display 36
Document (Draw) 60
Document (Paint) 74
Double Angle Brackets 135
Draw
    Palettes 54
    Text 52, 60
    Tools 52
Draw mode 51
Drop Cap 136
DTP 136
Duplicate (Draw) 58, 61
Duplicate (Paint) 71

E

Edit Button 25
Edition 34, 35
Enclosure 26

Enter 3, 15
Entry Bar 82
Entry Options 116
Excel 81, 87
Eyedropper 52

F

Field
    Active 101
    Calculation 110
    Date 103
    Number 103, 110
    Summary 112
File Transfer 125, 127
FileMaker Pro 99
Fill 57, 77
Fill Down 85, 92, 93
Find (Database)
    And 105
    New Request 105
    Or 105
    Request 104
Find/Change 33
Flip 77
Font 11, 38
    Adobe 38
    TrueType 38
Footnotes 30, 37
Formula 84, 85, 93, 97
Formula (Database) 110
Fractional Character Width 30
Frame 51, 130
    Open 44, 131
Frame Links 136
Functions 84, 90, 111, 142

G

Go to Cell 96
Go to Page 45

INDEX

Go to Record 102
Gradient Editor 55
Gradients 54
Grid 61, 62
Grid Lines (Spreadsheet) 97
Grid Size (Paint) 78
Group 62

H

Handles 52, 59
Header 9, 60, 74, 101
Header (Database) 101, 108
Help 17
    Balloons 17
Helvetica 11, 96
HyperCard 71
Hyphenate 32

I

I-Beam Pointer 9, 10, 60
Illustrator 53, 56
In Tray 27
Indent 12, 13
    First-Line 9, 13
    Hanging 13
Input List 116, 117
Insert 20
Insert Cells 95
Insert Date/Time/Page # 30
Insert Field 114
Insert Part 112
Insertion Point 9, 10
Install 4
Invert 77
Invisible Characters 15, 30

J

Justify 12

K

Key Chain 26
Keyboard 3

L

LaserWriter 75, 96
Layers 51, 63
Layout 106
    Columnar 107, 108
    Field 106
    Field Labels 106
    Field Order 107
    Labels 107, 109
    New 107
    Part Labels 106
    Parts 106
Layout Info 115
Lighter/Darker 71, 77
Line Spacing 11, 12, 13, 60
Link Indicator 137
Linked Frame 136
List View 114
Lock Title Position 97
Log Window 122

M

MacBinary 125
Macro 24, 39
    Edit Button 25
Mail 26
Mail Merge 134
Mailer 26
Make Chart 86
Make Default 23, 30
Margin 9
Margins 36, 44
Master Page 48, 61, 65

Match Records 119
Menus 146
    Apple 16
    Arrange 62
    Calculate 92
    Edit (Database) 114
    Edit (Draw) 58
    Edit (Spreadsheet) 90
    Edit (Text) 30
    File 18
    Font 38
    Format (Draw) 60
    Format (Paint) 74
    Format (Spreadsheet) 91
    Format (Text) 36
    Keys 127
    Layout 114
    Options (Draw) 64
    Options (Paint) 78
    Options (Spreadsheet) 96
    Organize 118
    Outline 40
    Session 126
    Settings 123
    Size 38
    Style 38
    Transform 76
    View 44
Microsoft Word 21, 134
Modem 121
Modify Arc 66
Modify Chart 86
Modify Frame 133
Mouse 2
Move Cells 92
Move Forward/Backward 63

N

Network 5
New 8, 19, 21, 100
New View 47
Not Enough Memory 69, 74
Number Format (Spreadsheet) 91

O

Object Info 64
Objects 51, 57
Open 20
Option 3
Option-Space 130
Outline
    Collapse 42
    Control Key 3
    Expand 42
    Formats 43
    Labels 43
    Topics 41
Outline View 40

P

Page Break (Spreadsheet) 96
Page guides 9, 36
Page Setup 28
Page View 29, 44
Pages (Draw) 60
Paint
    Frame 52, 70
    Frame Origin 75
    Text 70
    Tools 70
Paint mode 51, 69
Painting Mode 79
Palettes 54
Pane Tool 47

Paragraph 9, 12
Paste Special 90
Pattern Editor 55
Patterns 54
Pen Width 54
Perspective 76
Phone Book 122, 123
Phone Number 123
Pick Up 77
Piracy 5
Polygon Closing 58
PostScript 29
PowerTalk 26, 121
Precision 91
Preferences
    Com 122
    Graphics 58
    Mail 27
    Palette 23
    Text 30
Print 28, 75
Print Merge 135
Print Range 96
Publish/Subscribe 34

Q
QuickTime 49, 51, 66
Quit 18

R
RAM 69
Record 100
Registration 5
Reshape 59, 66
Resize 76
Resize Column/Row 83
Resolution and Depth 75
Return 3, 9
    Soft 15
Revert 18

Rotate 62
Rotate (Paint) 76
Round Corners 66
Row Headers 82
Row Height 83
Ruler 9, 12, 37, 44, 61, 74
    Apply 36
    Copy 36

S
Sample Documents 5
Save 19, 21
Save as 21
Scale 64
Scale (Draw) 56
Scan 75
Scrapbook 31
Scrollback 122
Select 10
Select (Draw) 52, 58
Select (Paint) 71
Select (Spreadsheet) 83
Shear 76
Shift Constraint 58
Shortcuts 3, 18, 22, 146
    Communication 127
    Database 118
    Draw 63
    Edit 22
    Paint 78
    Spreadsheet 92
    Text 15, 22
Show All Records 118
Size Palette 64
Slide Objects 109, 115
Slide Show 48
Smart Quotes 30

Smooth 57, 59
Sort Keys 94
Sort (Database) 108, 118
Sort (Spreadsheet) 94
Space Before/After 13
Spelling 32
Spray Can Editor 73, 78
Spreadsheet Mode 81
Stationery 8, 21
Status Area (Com) 122
Status Panel (Database) 101
Style 11
Sub-Summary Part 113
Subscribe 35
Subscript 11
Summary Part 112
Superscript 11
System 7 Pro 16, 26, 121

T
Tab 3, 12, 14, 29, 103
Tab Order 103, 115
Terminal Area 122
Terminal Settings 124
Text Overflow Indicator 137
Text Wrap 67
Thesaurus 32
Tint 79
Title Page 36
Tools 44, 45, 52, 70
    Arc 53
    Bezigon 53
    Brush 72
    Bucket 73
    Eraser 73
    Eyedropper 70
    Freehand 53, 57
    Lasso 71

    Magic Wand 71
    Oval 53, 57
    Pencil 70, 72
    Polygon 53
    Rectangle 53
    Select 71
    Spray Can 73
    Straight Line 53
    Zigzag 53, 57
Trailing Grand Summary 113
Transparent Pattern 79
Transpose 90
TTY 124
Tutorial 5

U
Undo 30
Untitled 19, 21

V
Verification 116
View Controls 9
View Scale 45
VT102 124

W
Windows
    Split 47
    Stack 46
    Tile 46
Word Processing 9
Wysiwyg 29

X
XModem 125

Z
Zoom 9, 45, 57